Kansas City

A Place in Time

D0889113

The preparation of this book was made possible through the generous support of Ozark National Life Insurance.

ISBN: 978-1-943338-13-9

Library of Congress Control Number: 2017939792

Published by Chandler Lake Books
2554 Chandler Road, Traverse City, Michigan

Printed in the United States of America by Walsworth Publishing Company, Marceline, Missouri.

Acknowledgements

Mayor Sylvester "Sly" James

The City Council of Kansas City, Missouri

Scott Wagner (Mayor Pro Tem)
Heather Hall
Teresa Loar
Dan Fowler
Quinton Lucas
Jermaine Reed
Katheryn Shields
Jolie Justus
Lee Barnes, Jr.
Alissia Canady
Scott Taylor
Kevin McManus

This book is dedicated to the life and legacy of Joelouis Mattox, who had the distinction of serving on the Historic Preservation Commission for more than 17 years and under five Kansas City mayors. Sadly, Joelouis passed on March 30, 2017, before he could see the completion of this book, which would not have been possible without the contributions he made as the commission's historian.

First appointed to the Landmarks Commission (now Historic Preservation Commission) in 1976, Joelouis Mattox worked alongside Jane Flynn, an instrumental leader in the development of Kansas City's historic preservation community. Like Jane Flynn, Joelouis Mattox was a mentor to many and he left an indelible impact on Kansas City. In 2008 Joe Louis Mattox was honored with the commissions' Jane Flynn Lifetime Achievement in Preservation Award.

Many of the buildings recognized in these pages will be remembered because of Joelouis Mattox's advocacy, particularly the buildings and sites that are significant to the African-American community. In his role as a commissioner, Joelouis Mattox was a consummate ambassador for the city he loved so much. His generous nature was evident in the way he always recognized properties that had reached or surpassed 100 years in age, thanking each applicant for their stewardship of our city's historic resources.

For those of us who had the good fortune of serving with Joelouis Mattox, I believe all would agree that Joe was the heart and soul of the Historic Preservation Commission. His deep knowledge of Kansas City and lifelong devotion to sharing this knowledge will be greatly missed.

Erik Heitman
Chairman, Historic Preservation Commission

Forty years ago, the Landmarks Commission of Kansas City, Missouri, published the first edition of A Place in Time not only as a guidebook, but as a way to preserve and promote the city's great wealth of history. Through the efforts of the (renamed) Historic Preservation Commission, the second edition's collection of landmarks and historic sites has been updated and now includes nearly twice as many significant properties.

The first and second edition's past and current committee members dedicated untold hours to selecting and revising locations, researching local sites, and writing – and rewriting – the words that follow this foreword.

The University of Missouri - Kansas City provided two interns, Matthew Reeves and Natalie Walker, who researched and updated new chapter introductions as well as numerous building descriptions.

City Planning and Development staff provided great input, editing, and support. Among those who gave their time were Director Jeffrey Williams, Kyle Elliott, Angela Eley, Chase Johnson and John Debauche.

However, among all the people I had the honor to work with on this project, the two who deserve the most credit are Bradley Wolf, the City Historic Preservation Officer, and Sheila Vemmer, Senior Planning Technician. Brad's tireless work ethic, fine-tuned historical research skills, institutional knowledge and professionalism greatly contributed to this project, while Sheila's technical skills and unbridled enthusiasm breathed life into a book that was many years in the making.

A special thank you is also due to Doug Weaver of Chandler Lake Books, whose expertise and local knowledge made it a smooth process in bringing this book to print.

I hope you enjoy this guide to some of Kansas City's greatest architectural and cultural achievements.

Mike Hardin
Vice Chairman, Historic Preservation Commission

First edition committee members included James Ryan, Kenneth E. Coombs, George Ehrlich, Vera Haworth Eldridge, David Boutros, Alberta Franciskato, Marjorie Kinney, Peggy Smith, Virginia Wright, Linda F. Becker, Victoria Karel, Edward J. Miszczuk, Elaine Ryder, Jane F. Flynn, Pamela S. Troxel and Melvin A. Solomon.

The National Register of Historic Places

The National Register of Historic Places records the story of our nation. It is a list of distinction identifying for the people those properties worthy of preservation for their architectural/historical values. Such properties are indicated by an arrowhead (the symbol of the National Parks Service.)

The Kansas City Register of Historic Places

The Kansas City Register of Historic Places records the story of our city. This is also a list of distinction identifying for the people those properties worthy of preservation for their architectural/historical values. Such properties found in this book are but a sampling of locally designated structures and are identified by the KC symbol.

This is a continuing process with the expectation that other significant Kansas City properties will be listed in both the National Register and Kansas City Register of Historic Places.

Contents

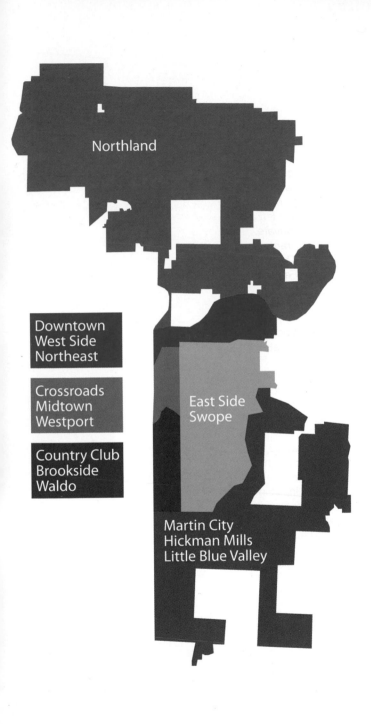

Northland

Downtown
West Side
Northeast

Crossroads
Midtown
Westport

Country Club
Brookside
Waldo

East Side
Swope

Martin City
Hickman Mills
Little Blue Valley

Introduction

This guidebook is a blend of architecture and history, presenting individual structures that chronicle the flow of time and people.

The reprint and expanded edition of A Place in Time retained many of the sites from the original publication, and added additional sites from new surveys as well as sites that have been identified since the original publication. While some choices may be debated, there are some buildings that are clearly significant for both architectural and historical values, while others are less apparently so. Surely no one would argue about the inclusion of the John B. Wornall House, an excellent example of Greek Revival architecture in the Midwest and one of the city's oldest surviving residences. On the other hand, the building that houses the Musician's Union Local 627 has few architectural attributes but is undeniably important as the home of Kansas City jazz. The Boley Building is an early example of a curtain-wall structure and its importance is primarily architectural.

The members of the Historic Preservation Commission Publication Committee, who made the selections, are acutely aware that many worthwhile structures have been omitted and recognize that not only would different individuals choose different buildings but that the same individuals might well choose differently another time.

The commission hopes to present examples of the many different structures in many areas of the city, not simply those of monumental quality. Equally important to the character of the city are the small neighborhood stores, the laborers' cottages, the factories and warehouses that were the basis of the city's wealth, the cemeteries, gas stations, and even historic trails. All of these sites give the city its texture and flavor.

Four goals motivated the compilation of this guidebook: to heighten awareness of the cityscape; to promote restoration or rehabilitation of existing buildings; to encourage reinvestment in some of the oldest sections of the city, which will be possible only if existing building stock is preserved; and to stimulate public interest in historic preservation.

The 319 square miles of Kansas City, Missouri, has been divided into six districts in this edition, unlike the eleven districts in the first edition. The evolution of these districts is attributable to a combination of physical, economic, and social forces. The Downtown/Westside/Northeast district contains many sites related to the emergence of Kansas City – the West Bottoms emerged as the site of warehouses and factories because it is flat and close to the rivers. Rail transportation followed, and industrial prosperity and changing lifestyles drove out thousands of dwellers. The Westside and Northeast areas developed residentially because of their rugged hills and beautiful views, and because settlement after the Civil War took an eastward direction. And the Downtown area has served as the governmental and economic center of Kansas City.

In some cases the location of one critical structure determined the course of surrounding development: the construction of the Union Station in the Midtown/Crossroads/Westport District stimulated certain types of building around it, even up to the present day; the town of Westport wasn't incorporated into Kansas City until 1897; the migration of the wealthy from Quality Hill (on the west end of downtown) to Hyde Park was the result of the lack of adjacent land in the Northeast area for expansion, the encroachment of commercial activities, and the allure of new and more fashionable areas.

The development of some districts can be explained in terms of technology. The automobile generated the seemingly unlimited expansion of Kansas City's boundaries as people were able to live farther from work. Others moved to avoid the traffic. The Country Club/Brookside/Waldo District reflects the growing importance of the automobile as housing transitioned from being dependent on the streetcar to having garages and driveways.

The East/Swope District reflects the rich heritage of Kansas City's African-American community. The 18th & Vine Historic District reflects the earliest remaining commercial and social center of the community and the Santa Fe District represents that era of the first push toward equal treatment in housing and social services. The area also contains the premier park of Kansas City, Swope Park, whose land was donated to the city by Colonel Swope in 1896.

The Northland and the Martin City/Hickman Mills/Little Blue District represent the post-World War II annexation areas. These areas were largely agricultural at the time and had towns such as Barry, Gashland, and Nashua up north and Martin City, Hickman Mills and Little Blue in the south. While these areas have supported, new development, they still retain the farmsteads, churches, school, cemeteries, and small commercial buildings related to that earlier agricultural heritage.

Kansas City's first architectural stirrings occurred at the beginning of the 19th century. On June 26, 1804, a party headed by Captains Meriwether Lewis and William Clark camped at the confluence of the Missouri and Kaw Rivers, later known as Kaw Point. Clark's journal records the construction of a barrier to protect the men and boats: "A strong redoubt or brest work from (one) river to the other, of logs and bushes six feet high." One historical researcher deemed this the record of the earliest construction by non-Indians within the present metropolitan area.

In 1821, the year that Missouri entered the Union, Francois Chouteau of St. Louis received authorization to establish a trading center with the Kansa, Osage, and other tribes near the junction of the Missouri and Kansas Rivers. Chouteau spear-headed a small French settlement later to become Kansas City. In 1826, when a period of Indian removal was coming to an end, Jackson County was chartered and Independence was founded as the county seat. Independence prospered on the Santa Fe trade and Indian annuities. Its success inspired the founding of other communities nearby.

In 1834, John Calvin McCoy, a surveyor and merchant, filed a plat of a town he named Westport, 11 miles west of Independence and 2 miles from the frontier. Rather than haul goods from Independence via a difficult and often flooded trail, he arranged for a steamboat to unload on a natural levee near what is now the foot of Grand Avenue. Goods delivered there were hauled overland to McCoy's general store in Westport, an outfitting center for the Oregon and Santa Fe Trails.

McCoy organized the Kansas Town Company in 1838 and managed to buy the landing itself. At first called Kansas, this became the Town of Kansas, then the City of Kansas, and in 1889, was chartered as Kansas City. The warehouses, stores, and taverns that sprang up on this landing soon eclipsed the neighboring town of Westport that had justified their existence.

Both Westport and the City of Kansas thrived in the 1850s despite the ominous rumblings of border warfare. But the effects of the Civil War were calamitous. Westport never fully recovered and the City of Kansas emerged down at the heel and with a loss of population.

However, in 1865 the Missouri-Pacific Railroad reached Kansas City, and thanks to a united and determined citizenry, in 1869 the city managed to span the Missouri River with the crucial Hannibal Bridge. A measure of the town's vitality is to be found in the growth of its population, which between 1865 and 1870 surged from 6,000 to 30,000,

By 1870 the city, like many in America, turned its back on the river. The bluffs were graded and the ravines were filled. Streets were cut through to the south. The 1880s was a boom decade with extensive residential construction, a growing business district, and cable car lines connecting the city's north and south reaches.

After several recessions, the 1890s saw continued expansion and development of an overall plan for the city's growth. This plan recommended establishment of an extensive park and boulevard system for Kansas City and was presented in the 1893 report of the city's Board of Park and Boulevard Commissioners.

This early example of integrated citywide planning called for four major parks connected by a network of boulevards, which defined and separated industrial, commercial, and residential sections. The plan served to generate and preserve property values, providing an incentive for quality residential development and encouraging planned land use. Four additional goals were achieved: to combine aesthetics with utility; to preserve the natural topography and forestation; to replace blighted areas; and to provide recreational facilities. The oldest sections of the system were listed on the National Register of Historic Places in 2016.

The period from 1900 to 1910 saw skyscrapers thrust into the Kansas City skyline and the completion of plans for a new Union Station to be located south of downtown. The ensuing years combined turbulence and progress: political turmoil in the 1920s, depression in the 1930s, war in the 1940s, and suburban expansion in the 1950s and 1960s. In the 1970s a growing interest in the city's past has become apparent. When this book was first published, the Folly Theater was under restoration, and subsequently became a premier performing arts venue in Kansas City.

When the city adopted its current comprehensive plan, FOCUS, it adopted a specific section for historic preservation known as A Plan for Meaningful Communities. At the time of publication, there are more than 2,300 properties on the Kansas City Register of Historic Places and more than 4,400 on the National Register of Historic Places. The commission

wishes to continue these great strides by surveying and identifying historic properties in the other portions of the city. The
members of the Historic Preservation Commission endorse
these endeavors and hope this guidebook will reinforce the
trend, preserving our architectural and cultural past as a living
part of the community.

**Downtown
West Side
Northeast**

River Market

1. Second Hannibal Bridge
2. Townley Metal Co.
3. Morgan Drug Co.
4. George M. Shelley
   Dry Goods Co.
5. The Ebenezer Building
6. Pacific House Hotel
7. The City Market
8. Horton's Oyster & Chop House
9. Helping Hand Institute
10. Cold Storage Building
11. Metropolitan Street Railway
    Power Plant

West Bottoms

12. Live Stock Exchange Building
13. Kansas City Drovers
    Telegram Co.
14. Fairbanks, Morse & Co.
15. John Deere Plow Co.
16. Studebaker Brothers Mfg. Co.
17. West Bottoms
    Commercial Buildings
18. Richards & Conover
    Hardware Co.
19. Bliss Syrup & Preserving Co.
20. Ryley, Wilson & Co.
21. Ridenour, Baker & Co.
22. C. A. Murdock Mfg. Co.
23. Fire Station No. 1
24. Crooks Terminal Building
25. 12th Street Viaduct

Quality Hill

26. George Blossom Residence
27. Grace & Holy Trinity Cathedral
28. Standard (Folly) Theater
29. Cathedral of the
    Immaculate Conception
30. Coates House Hotel
31. James E. Fitzpatrick Saloon

Downtown

32. Warehouse (Garment) District
33. Builders & Traders
    Exchange Building
34. Savoy Hotel & Grill
35. Baker-Vawter Building
36. Historic Financial
    (Library) District
37. New England Building
38. Bunker & McEwen Building
39. New York Life Building
40. Hotel Phillips
41. Muehlebach Hotel
42. Midland Office Building
    Midland Theater Building
43. Municipal Auditorium

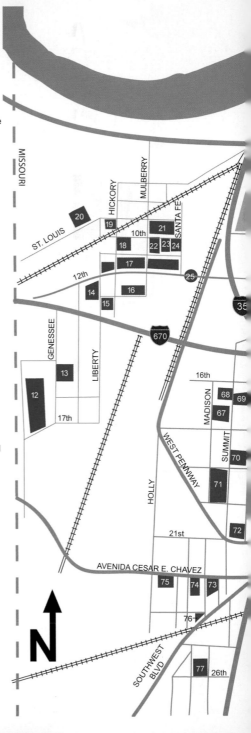

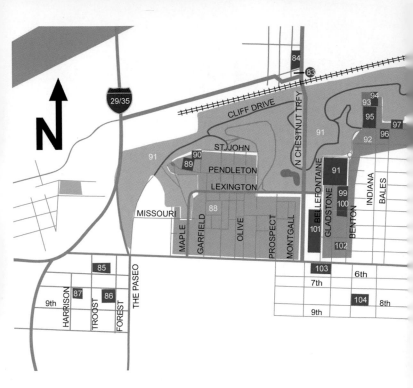

East Bottoms

83. Heim Fire Station No. 20
84. Heim Brewery Bottling Plant

85. Eighth Street Residences
86. First Church of Christ, Scientist
87. Masonic Temple

Northeast

88. Pendleton Heights
89. Phillip E. Chapell Residence
90. Flavel B. Tiffany Residence
91. Cliff Drive & North Terrace Park (Kessler Park)
92. Scarritt Point District
93. William Wallace District
94. William Chick Scarritt Residence
95. R.A. Long Residence - Corinthian Hall
96. Mrs. Harvey A. Brower Residence
97. Judge Edward L. Scarritt Residence
98. Calvert Hunt Residence
99. Heim Brothers Residences
100. Benton Boulevard Streetscape

101. Bellefontaine Avenue District
102. Milo E. Lawrence Residence
103. Independence Boulevard Christian Church
104. Lutheran Church of Our Redeemer
105. Oakley Methodist Episcopal Church
106. Northeast High School
107. Montgomery Ward Building
108. The "Alligator" House

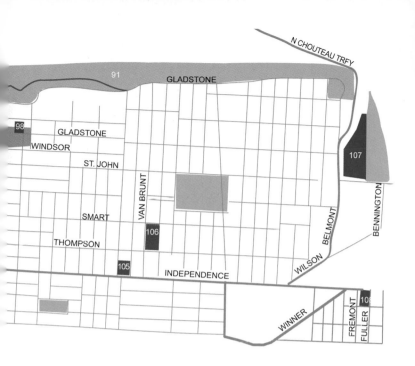

Downtown
Westside
Northeast

It all began with the rivers, their intersection, and a push for new land and opportunity. From the River Market to Downtown, out through the West Bottoms and back to the Northeast Side, modern visitors can trace the tumult of urbanization and industrialization. Wealth, created by industry, turned into sky scraping steel. As those business buildings went upward, laborers and their families moved outward, into new communities formed specifically to meet the industry's needs. The variety of building sizes and styles reflected each neighborhood's distinct class and ethnic characteristics. Kansas City's diverse spectrum of built human environments immediately south of the Missouri river – trading ports, industrial parks, business districts, and residential neighborhoods – narrates local history in a way that no human being can.

Kansas City was born of the river. The riverfront district's street grid, aligned with the Missouri River, reminds visitors that transportation and trade on America's waterways dictated early patterns of migration and commerce. Originally platted as "Kansas," the nascent community survived floods in 1833 and 1844 and cholera epidemics in 1848 through 1850. Town Square, the community's original business center, maintained its commercial character throughout the years, eventually becoming widely known to modern visitors as the City Market. The area experienced massive demographic growth in the late antebellum years, as the population ballooned from 700 in 1854 to more than 5,000 in 1857. The coming hostilities, both local and national, had a chilling effect on trade and migration. Though the Civil War had little direct impact on the area's architecture, the conflict's indirect effects – stagnation and deterioration – damaged the previously booming business economy.

The antebellum Town of Kansas grew from the river trade, but City of Kansas emerged from the ability to cross the river by rail. In the years following the Civil War, local business leaders and real estate speculators Kersey Coates and Robert Van Horn convinced the federal government that the City of Kansas was the ideal place for a Missouri river railroad crossing. The Hannibal Bridge (1869) subsequently assured that transcontinental freight and passenger transportation passed through the City of Kansas. The resulting commercial and economic boom spurred a flurry of construction, visible in the red brick Italianate and Romanesque Revival buildings saturating the business districts surrounding the Riverfront district, and the residential buildings built predominately for Italian immigrant families in the North End.

And the growth was just beginning, as the city's commercial needs pushed south into an area that would become known as the Central Business District. Between 1869, when Kersey Coates opened the Coates House Hotel on the newly created Broadway, and 1894, when the city began grading Grand Avenue, the Central Business District underwent an unprecedented period of growth. The New York Life Insurance Company acknowledged the city's swelling national profile when it built its regional headquarters at 9th and Baltimore in 1887. Other major business concerns followed New York Life, and as the buildings went up, so did the population. By 1880, the city had 56,000 residents; a sizable amount, but nothing compared to 1890, when the population more than doubled to 133,000. In 1889, the booming urban center adopted a new charter, officially changing its name to Kansas City.

Though businesses like New York Life chose Kansas

City as a regional business hub, the city's driving economic force was the livestock trade. Industrial barons could look west from the heights of their new skyscrapers in the Central Business District, tracing the rocky cliffs westward down into the West Bottoms. A massive expanse of stockyards, towering red brick Romanesque factories, and modest workers cottages, the West Bottoms were the industrial engine that powered Kansas City's commercial machine. The western territories produced beef in much greater quantities than they could consume, shipping their surplus cattle east to Kansas City. Technological innovations like the refrigerated railroad car allowed for cattle processed in Kansas City to then travel on to great urban centers in the east. The architecture in the West Bottoms hints at the optimism and opulence of the period, apparent in the terra cotta medallions, ornamental rams-head sculptures, and decorative arches that adorn otherwise pragmatic factory and warehouse structures.

All this industrial and commercial growth created a demand for labor, and those employees in turn needed housing. Proximity to their workplaces, along with emerging class divides, dictated where workers settled. Quality Hill, a tony neighborhood south of the river and west of downtown, developed in lock step with the central business district and served as the upper class destination address for much of the late nineteenth-century. Characterized by their French-colonial style, the upscale homes perched on limestone bluffs took in spectacular views of the West Bottoms. The neighborhood is also home to the Cathedral of the Immaculate Conception (1883). Built on the highest ground in the city, the cathedral's golden-leaf cupola was visible throughout the burgeoning metropolis.

As the city grew, the residential neighborhoods pushed south from Quality Hill into what became the Westside – an area west of Midtown and east of the bluffs that separated the city from the West Bottoms. Residents were predominately working class and of Irish and mixed European ancestry, and most of the houses were pattern homes, erected without the assistance of an architect. But building from a pattern did not mean cookie-cutter repetition. Westside homes near the bluffs display remarkable variety. Two-story asymmetrical brick houses were interspersed with one-story frame houses and brick cottages. One common style – characterized by a central gable on the front façade – became so popular that it was widely known as "Kansas City Peaked Style." After the turn of the century, the Westside's ethnic character changed, as railroad recruiting drew a growing population of Mexican-Americans to Kansas City. Our Lady of Guadalupe, the Westside's first Mexican-American parish, was dedicated in 1914.

While the Westside's development was influenced by its proximity to the West Bottoms, independent business communities shaped the land northeast of the Central Business District. The neighborhood's geography mirrored the land to west, as elevated properties closer to the city center gave away to low lying river bottoms. The German immigrant Heim Family established a brewery in the East Bottoms in 1901. Up the bluffs from the brewery, formerly independent manufacturing communities like Sheffield and Manchester officially became part of Kansas City. Growth added diversity, both in terms of ethnic character from the largely German East Bottoms, and business variety from Sheffield and Manchester.

Kansas City leaders' efforts to create a "City Beautiful" consciously shaped civic development in the Northeast.

Local landowner Nathan Scarritt, a farmer and Methodist minister, played a pivotal role in this development. His families' decision to donate land for North Terrace Park (1893) was integral to the implantation of urban planner George Kessler's grand design for Kansas City. North Terrace Park served as an anchor park for planned system of grand boulevards that would link the northeast to the rest of the city. Under the leadership of August R. Meyer, the first president of the Kansas City Park Board, the city constructed a major north-south artery. Meyer, who made his fortune from Mexican mines, named the thoroughfare The Paseo after Mexico City's beautiful Paseo de la Reforma. With its place in the City Beautiful plan assured, the Northeast also gained a reputation as a magnificent residential neighborhood. Affluent families flocked to the area, drawn by its beauty and easy access to the newly constructed network of boulevards. Ornate residences were the standard for the area, but Robert Long's mansion at 3218 Gladstone Boulevard stood out from the rest. Decorated in the Beaux Arts style, the Long's Mansion - christened Corinthian Hall (1911) - is today the home of the Kansas City Museum.

Kansas City's development was intimately tied to the river. From the first traders and pioneers it brought to the region, all the way to the railroad bridge that crossed here, ensuring Kansas City's continued prominence, the river left an indelible mark on Kansas City. Its influence stretched from the Riverfront District out to the indus-trial West Bottoms and up the bluffs to the Westside; it brought the wealth that created the concrete canyons of the Central Business District, the palaces of the North-east, and the brewers in the East Bottoms. Though each neighborhood had its own particular architectural idiom, they all in some sense flowed from the river.

Second Hannibal Bridge

1

1915-1917

Chief Engineer:
C.H. Cartlidge, Chicago

Builder (Superstructure):
American Bridge Co., Chicago

The construction of the first Hannibal Bridge was deemed one of the most important events in Kansas City history. It placed this city, rather than Leavenworth, Atchison or St. Joseph, at the junction of railroad lines to Chicago, St. Louis, the West and Southwest, thus determining Kansas City's future as a metropolis and the gateway to the Southwest.

The original bridge, designed by Octave Chanute, was built by the Hannibal and St. Joseph Railroad line. It opened July 3, 1869, with a celebration that included parades, bands, speeches, cannon fire, and a balloon ascension. The bridge's wooden structures were replaced with steel in 1889, and in 1917 an entirely new bridge was opened, just 200 feet west of the old bridge. Until 1956, this bridge carried both rail and motor car traffic. However, during the 1950s the motor car level became increasingly congested, leading to the construction of yet another bridge, the Broadway Bridge. The traffic deck of the Hannibal Bridge was closed in 1956 and was later removed altogether.

Townley Metal Co.

218 Delaware Street
c. 1890

Builder:
Schoen Brothers

The Romanesque style, a unique American revival,
is typified in the arches of the facade of this building.
Stoves, tin, tinner supplies, and roofing plates were sold
from this building by the Townley Metal Company, the
original owner.

Morgan Drug Co.

302-304 Delaware Street
c. 1869

These brick Italianate style buildings with cast iron fronts and rhythmic semicircular arched windows were both erected around 1869. The earliest known merchant located in these buildings was W. H. Morgan and Company, a wholesale drug firm. Both buildings form part of one of the few surviving commercial streetscapes from the 19th century.

George M. Shelley Dry Goods Co.
306-308 Delaware Street
c. 1870

Cast iron lintels enhance the distinguished red brick facades of these buildings, once the home of the exclusive
George M. Shelley Dry Goods Company. Known as "The
Merchant of Delaware Street," Shelley came to Kansas
City in 1868; in 1878, when he was 29, he was elected
mayor and served two terms. He was considered an
energetic and progressive mayor.

To promote a new sewer system, Shelley urged City
Council members to don "sou'westers" and rubber coats.
With Shelley in the lead, they entered a sewer at 3rd and
Walnut Streets and crawled on hands and knees to 10th
and Walnut Streets.Shortly thereafter, Shelley's recom-
mendations were enacted.

The Ebenezer Building

5

309 Delaware Street
c. 1890

Having originally housed the William W. Kendall Boot and Shoe Company, this five-story red brick building is especially notable for its three elaborately decorated terra cotta gables. Kendall sold "ladies' and misses' shoes and gents' shoes and gaiters" that had been manufactured in nearby Leeds. Adjoining on the south is the four-story Ebenezer Addition, built to house the Benedict Paper Company.

Pacific House Hotel

401 Delaware Street
1860; 1868

Architect:
Asa Beebe Cross

Builder:
John and Robert Hall

This three-story brick hotel was considered the finest hostelry in the city until the late 1880s when newer hotels were constructed to the south. Its designer, Asa Beebe Cross, was one of Kansas City's earliest and finest architects. The hotel was occupied from 1861 to 1865 by Union troops, and it was here in 1863 that General Thomas Ewing issued his famous Order No. 11, in which all residents of Jackson County who refused to give allegiance to the United States government were forced to abandon their homes and fields.

Frank and Jesse James were said to have been frequent visitors in the hotel, playing billiards and lounging about the bar.

The City Market

5th Street and Walnut Street
1939-1940

Architect:
Frederick C. Gunn

Builder:
Thomas D. Bryant

The present three-story buff brick buildings are located on a site that has served the public as a city hall and market square since the 1840s. In 1857, two merchants were given permission to operate stalls. The first covered stalls were erected in 1888, permitting year-round market sales. Even though the population pushed farther south, the market continued to thrive.

In 1940 it was estimated to be a $25 million a year business, and in 1975 there were estimated sales of $92 million. Today second or third generations still sell produce from stalls started by their families at the turn of the century.

Horton's Oyster & Chop House 8

507 Walnut Street

c. 1879

This red brick building, now painted white, features a checkerboard brick design within the spandrels and an elaborate metal entablature. A periodical of the day commented that this eating place "is very popular with leading businessmen of the section." The building to the north, 505 Walnut Street, is a fine example of tapestry brick design.

Helping Hand Institute

523 Grand Boulevard
1915

9

Architect:
Smith, Rea & Lovitt

Builder:
George L. Brown & Sons

Men and women down on their luck could find a bath, a meal, a bed, and religious inspiration in this five-story building. The Helping Hand Institute founded in the 1890s was "...not to be a loafing palace for the chronic jobless but a modern institution designed to aid the temporary down-and-outer to rise again by self help." The Institute continues to serve the city today and offers help to those needing assistance.

Cold Storage Building

416 East 3rd Street
1922; add. 1927

Architect:
S. Scott Joy

The Cold Storage building is a 365,000-square-foot structure adjacent to an abandoned spur of the Kansas City Southern Railroad. The building is an excellent example of a railroad-related commercial-distribution property. The reinforced concrete structure has red brick walls and terracotta accents. While the cubic massing and largely blank walls reflect the building's historic industrial function, the terracotta trim and gargoyles that encircle the building's upper story reference Jacobethan/ Tudor Revival architectural styling.

The building's history reflects a calculated expansion of the cold storage industry by outside investors. The investors capitalized on the city's role as a regional and national rail hub to accentuate its position in the national ice, fruit, and vegetable markets. The resource is a unique example of a commercial cold storage facility due to its large size and strategic location adjacent to the 2nd Street railroad corridor and the wholesale produce operation in the Old Town industrial district.

Metropolitan Street Railway Power Plant

115 Grand Boulevard
1903; adds. 1914,1930,1954

This plant was originally constructed to provide the power to operate one of the city's street railway systems, the Metropolitan Street Railway Company. Bernard Corrigan, head of the company, earlier controlled seven of the city's horse car lines. He converted the lines into a cable system in 1886. After gasoline-powered transportation supplanted the cable cars, this plant continued to provide power for the Kansas City Electric Light Company.

Live Stock Exchange Building
1600 Genessee Street
1910

Architect:
Wilder & Wight

Builder:
Swenson Construction Co.

A trade journal wrote, "Rapid growth and development of the stockyards contributed to the construction of the Live Stock Exchange Building, the largest building in the world devoted to live stock interests." The size of this nine-story brick office building is indicative of the importance of the livestock industry, which was a cornerstone of the growth of Kansas City from 1867, when the first cattle were shipped from Texas to the city for feeding and watering.

Kansas City Drovers Telegram Co.

1505 Genessee Street
1909; add. 1946

Architects:
Herman J. Stroeh (1909)
George Fuller Green (1946)

Builder:
Hollinger Construction

A pair of ornately carved rams' heads contrasts with the tailored design of this buff brick and cut stone office building. This is one of the few buildings in the area where the ground floor facade has not been remodeled. Until 1970 this building housed *The Kansas City Drovers Telegram*, a newspaper for stockmen that was published daily until 1964 when it became a weekly.

Fairbanks, Morse & Co.

1216 Liberty Street
1907

Architect:
James Oliver Hogg

The front of this five-story building with glazed terra cotta panels shows reliefs of figures bearing banners with the word "Advance." This word was part of the original firm name, Advance Thrasher Company, which assembled oil pull tractors. From about 1915 to 1959, the building was a warehouse for Fairbanks, Morse and Company.

John Deere Plow Co.

1401 West 13th Street
1890; add. 1898

Architect:
Root & Siemens (1898)

A second-floor bay window on the east side of the build-ing provided a touch of elegance to this red brick and terra cotta warehouse and office. The arched entrance framing the recessed doorway represents a 1902 remod-eling. When erected, this building housed the warehouse offices and salesrooms for the vehicles and agricultural implements basic to the farmland industry of the Mid-west.

Studebaker Brothers Manufacturing Co.

1320 West 13th Street
1903

Architect:
Root & Siemens

Builder:
Taylor & Winn

The Studebaker Brothers Manufacturing Company built this nine-story Neoclassical red brick building enhanced with terra cotta and cut stone to be used as a general office and warehouse for its carriages, buggies and wagons. Stowe Hardware & Supply Company has occupied the building since 1918.

West Bottoms Commercial Buildings

1200-1418 West 12th Street

Appearing overshadowed by the 12th Street Viaduct, these vigorous red brick buildings form one of the last remaining intact and unaltered rows of late 19th century commercial structures in Kansas City. Constructed side by side like fashionable townhouses, they housed some of Kansas City's leading industries, including implement businesses, warehouses, and paint and wholesale grocery companies.

K.C. Bolt, Nut & Screw Co.
Adriance Van Brunt, 1900

Deere, Mansur & Co.
c. 1894

Richards & Conover Hardware Co. 18

1331 Union Avenue
1885

Architect:
Foster & Liebbe, Des Moines, Iowa

This red brick warehouse was designed with an angled corner, corbelled parapet and a cast-iron front, a popular architectural device of the period. The firm of Richards and Conover, founded in 1857, whose offices and sales-rooms were at 5th and Walnut Streets warehoused its scales, safes, saws, tin ware, barbed wire, springs, and axles here.

Bliss Syrup & Preserving Co.

1331 St. Louis Avenue
1897

This sturdy brick building with its handsome cornice, anchors and rusticated first story was constructed to house the Bliss Syrup Refining Company, founded about 1883 to refine and distribute syrups, molasses, preserves, jellies, fruit butters, marmalades and jams. An 1892 sketch commented, "This company has an immense trade throughout the west, selling to merchants as far west as the Pacific Coast, and the east to the Mississippi River. It is the largest and most important company in the business."

Ryley, Wilson & Co.

1500 St. Louis Avenue
1887

Multiple arches and handsome cut brick details make this an exceptional building. This wholesale grocery business, established in the 1880s, sold to retail groceries in the area such as Miller's Grocery, 1301 Union Avenue, which catered to the Union Depot passengers.

Ridenour, Baker & Co.

933 Mulberry Street
1915

Architect:
McKecknie & Trask

Reinforced concrete was a new building material at the time of construction of this warehouse and was used for the exterior of this building. The concrete medallions atop the vertical members are typical of the decorative elements of this period and were usually rendered in terra cotta; they are similar to some decorative motifs on the Montgomery Ward building located in the Northeast District. This warehouse was constructed for Ridenour, Baker and Company, grocers, founded in 1858. It was later known as the Kansas City Terminal Warehouse Building.

C.A. Murdock Mfg. Co.

1225 Union Avenue
1887

The powerful arches of this commercial building are
typical of many late 19th century business structures in
Kansas City. C. A. Murdock Manufacturing Company,
a leading importer "of the choicest select coffees and
spices with all roasting, grinding, and packing done
directly on the premises," contributed exotic aromas to
delight visitors in the area.

Fire Station No. 1

1215 Union Avenue
1927-1928

Architect:
Michael J. O'Connor

Builder:
Jason F. Dunn

This handsome buff brick and terra cotta fire station replaced an earlier station in this district. In the city's early
years, cisterns dug in the middle of the streets constitut-
ed the source of water supply used in fighting fires. After
a fire was out, firemen had to go to the nearest lake or
pond and pump water back into the cistern to be ready
for the next fire. Stations were equipped with fire bells
that could be heard 10 or 15 miles away.

Crooks Terminal Building

1209 Union Avenue
1930-1931

Architect:
The Walters Co., Chicago

Builder:
W.K. Martin Construction Co.

The Crooks Company, a public warehouse firm, was founded in Chicago in 1913 and opened its Kansas City division in 1922. In 1930, Crooks Terminal Warehouse erected this Art Deco red brick warehouse. The warehouse is notable for its decorative use of buff brick around the windows and cut stone and fan motifs bracketing the entrance.

12ᵗʰ Street Viaduct

12th Street between Hickory Street and I-35
1915

Architect:
Waddell & Harrington

Builder:
Groff Construction Co., Seattle

Railroads, skirting the city's troublesome bluffs, converged in the West Bottoms and introduced the problem of moving people and goods between the railway terminal below and the downtown district above. A circuitous road was the only route between the differing elevations until 1885, when cable lines were built.

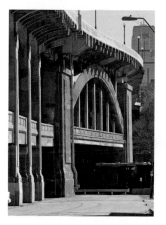

The 12ᵗʰ Street Viaduct, the first direct roadway between the bluff top and river bottom, opened in 1915. A widely acclaimed engineering feat, the 12ᵗʰ Street Viaduct was built as a double deck reinforced concrete bridge, inclined at a moderate slope.

Completely rebuilt in 1965, the upper deck is now a four-lane thoroughfare.

George Blossom Residence

26

1032 Pennsylvania Avenue
1888

Architect:
Van Brunt & Howe

Builder:
Norcross Brothers, Worcester, Mass.

This residence was built for George Blossom, owner of the Blossom House, a famous Union Avenue hotel in the West Bottoms. Constructed of brick with terra cotta trim and sandstone lintels and sills, it is one of the few remaining grand houses in the Quality Hill area.

Grace & Holy Trinity Cathedral

415 West 13th Street
1888-1889; adds. 1894,1934

Architects:
Adriance Van Brunt & Co. (1888)
F.E. Hill (1894)
Wight & Wight (1934)

Constructed in Neo-Norman transitional style, Grace
and Holy Trinity Cathedral is both an architectural and
ecclesiastical amalgamation. Architecturally, the cathedral was constructed in three distinct phases. The parish
hall, designed by Van Brunt and built in 1889, was the
first completed section of the church. Two years later
the nave was constructed based on a design by F. E.
Hill. The last element, the tower, was completed in 1938.
Designed by renowned Kansas City architects Wight &
Wight, the tower's style matched the much older parish
hall and nave. In addition to its striking architecture, the
cathedral features exceptional Tiffany stained glass windows, and an elaborate Tiffany rood screen separates
the nave from the chancel.

Standard (Folly) Theater

28

300 West 12th Street
1900

Architect:
Louis S. Curtiss

Builder:
R.P. McClure Construction Co.
(St. Louis)

An important example of turn-of-the-century theater architecture, the Standard Theater is a reminder of the age of legitimate theater in Kansas City. Playbills boasted names such as Al Jolson and Fannie Brice, and boxer Jack Dempsey once fought a bout in the theater. In 1941 it opened as the Folly, a burlesque theater, with appearances by burlesque stars such as Gypsy Rose Lee.

Cathedral of the Immaculate Conception

407 West 11th Street
1882-84

Architect:
T.R. Tinsley

Builder:
Seddon, Taylor & Co.

The steady growth of the Cathedral of the Immaculate Conception mirrored the growing Catholic population in Kansas City. John Joseph Hogan, bishop of the newly created Kansas City Diocese, selected the cathedral's site in 1880. Built of brick and cut stone, the four-story Romanesque structure replaced a smaller preexisting parish church. The cathedral celebrated its first mass in 1882, and the local community added a seven-bell carillon in 1892. Elaborate stained-glass windows dated from 1912, a gift from the parish and the product of local craftsmen.

Built on one of the highest points in downtown Kansas City, the cathedral dominated the local skyline in the years before high rises and skyscrapers. In an effort to recover some of that lost distinctiveness, Bishop Cody had the cathedral's aging copper cupola renovated and covered in gold leaf in 1960.

Coates House Hotel

1005 Broadway Boulevard
1886-1887; adds.1889-1891; rehab. 1980

Architect:
Van Brunt & Howe

Builder:
C.E. Clarke, Boston

The present hotel occupies the site of the original Coates House Hotel, built on land purchased in 1855 by Kersey Coates, an early Kansas City entrepreneur. The original hotel was replaced by the present building, constructed in two major phases with a gala opening in 1891. Many notables patronized this once fashionable hotel, including former Presidents Grover Cleveland and Theodore Roosevelt. The south third of the hotel was destroyed by fire in 1978.

James E. Fitzpatrick Saloon

931 Broadway Boulevard
1911

Architect:
Thurtle & Thayer

Builder:
Flanagan Brothers

Constructed as a saloon serving patrons from the nearby Quality Hill Neighborhood, this three-story tapestry brick building most notably features a prominent two-story copper window bay and crowing brick parapet. The first floor originally served as the bar while the upper floors housed a brothel.

With the advent of Prohibition in 1919, alcohol could no longer be consumed openly, yet Kansas City social life continued. Spirits and other contraband moved to the basement, where the speakeasy was a popular unofficial meeting place for the city's local elite. Some patrons made use of the discrete alley entrance and a tunnel leading to the opera house next door. The saloon also received the unofficial sanction of political players like "Boss" Tom Pendergast. Local government was unconcerned with enforcing Prohibition, a libertine attitude that help the city earn the nickname "The Paris of the Plains."

Warehouse (Garment) District

306-423 West 8th Street

1888-1930

Architects:

306-310 William W. Rose

307 James C. Sunderland

312 A. Van Brunt & Bros.

313-323 George Mathews

330 Shepard & Farrar

405-409

407

412 Shepard & Farrar

423

Builder:

George L. Brown & Son

Burt Dyche

George L. Brown & Son

George L. Brown & Son

John T. Neil

George L. Brown & Son

George L. Brown & Son

Stroeh, Brown & Germain

The majority of the masonry and steel buildings on these two blocks were constructed over the span of a decade. The design of these buildings, which range in scale from five to eight stories, were greatly influenced by the architectural innovations that had come out of Chicago. Consisting of warehouses and factories, these buildings reflected Kansas City's vast jobbing and wholesale markets at the turn of the century, and developed into one of the busiest distribution centers in the country for manufactured goods.

Builders & Traders Exchange Building

616 Central Street
1889

Architect:
Knox & Guinotte

Offices used exclusively for members of the Builders & Traders Exchange, including architects, contractors, builders and others involved in the building trade, were provided within this imposing five-story structure. The building was designed and constructed by various members of the Builders &Traders Exchange.

Savoy Hotel & Grill

219 West 9th Street
c. 1888; add. 1898-1900

Architects:
S.E. Chamberlain
Van Brunt & Howe (add.)

Builders:
Schnick, Massman & Flanagan
S.J. Hayde Construction Co. (add.)

Representative of a past period of elegance, this turn-of-the-century hotel and restaurant catered to the tastes of Kansas City's fashionable society. The Classical Revival design features stylized leaded windows designed by Frank Anderson, representing an exceptional and rare example of the Art Nouveau influence in America.

Baker-Vawter Building

915 Wyandotte Street
1920

Architect:
Hoit, Price & Barnes

Builder:
Long Construction Co.

One of the earliest commercial designs by the Kansas City architecture firm Hoit, Price & Barnes, the Baker-Vawter Building serves as one of the best surviving examples of interwar industrial architecture in Kansas City. The Baker-Vawter Company manufactured perpetual ledgers, commercial ordering systems, and filing cabinetry – the advanced business equipment of the time.

Visually, the Baker-Vawter Building combines pragmatics and stylistic design. The six-story brick structure's primary façade features terra cotta veneers and a decorative pediment featuring intricate terra cotta design work. Three bays of large industrial windows dominate the façade, offering efficient ventilation. Pilasters frame the window bays, adding a Neoclassical element to the design. These decorative flourishes enhance the front façade, adding stylistic elements to an otherwise pragmatic manufacturing building.

Historic Financial (Library) District 36
9th Street & Baltimore Avenue

The Library District is a modern neighborhood organized in 2003 when the Central Branch of the Kansas City Public Library relocated to the historic First National Bank Building (1880). The district includes several buildings on the National Register of Historic Places. Many of these structures have been repurposed, including the New York Life Building, which now houses the administrative offices for the Roman Catholic Diocese of Kansas City-St. Joseph and the local branch of Catholic Charities.

Like the Wholesale District, the Library District has a lengthy period of significance; buildings in the district date from 1880-1931. This broad range spans many architectural styles and movements. Consider the New England Building (1886), an example of ornate late nineteenth-century Renaissance Revival, and the nearby Carbide and Carbon Building (1931), which typifies Art Deco style. Separated by fifty years and by substantial differences in style, these two buildings exemplify the Library District's valuable architectural diversity. Using the Library's Central Branch as an anchor tenant, the rejuvenated district continues to attract individual visitors, business relocations, and residential adaptive reuse.

Wood's Building/Hotel Cosby, 1881
100-107 West 9th Street

First National Bank
14 West 10th Street
1904-1906

Architects:
Wilder & Wight
Wight & Wight (west add.)
Marshall & Brown (north add.)

Builder:
George L. Brown & Son

Carbide and Carbon Building
912 Baltimore Avenue
1930-1931

Architect:
William Bovard

Builder:
University Building Co.

New England Building

112 West 9th Street
1886-1888

Architects:
Bradlee, Winslow & Wetherell, Boston
with Van Brunt & Howe

As a show of faith by eastern investors in the potential business future of Kansas City, this handsome brownstone Italian Renaissance style building was constructed to house the New England Mutual Life Insurance Company. Along the southwest corner of the structure is its most distinguishing feature, a two-story-high oriel bay ornamented with the five carved seals of the New England states.

Bunker & McEwen Building

100 West 9th Street
1881

This four-story red brick building is situated amid a cluster of buildings that formed a part of the business/financial center of Kansas City in the late 19th century. The Lyceum Building, 104 West 9th Street, and the former Kansas City Dime Museum at 110 West 9th Street, also formed part of that center. The construction of the Bunker Building was partially financed by Walter A. Bunker, founder of the Western Newspaper Union. Bunker was also a staff member of the Kansas City Journal and an ardent promoter of Kansas City.

New York Life Building

20 West 9th Street
1887-90

Architects:
McKim, Mead & White
with F.E. Hill and Van Brunt & Howe

The beauty of this brownstone, masonry and terra cotta structure is enhanced by the imposing bronze eagle, cast in the studio of Augustus Saint-Gaudens. Upon completion, it was the largest building in the city and was a decisive departure from the prevailing Richardsonian Romanesque style used in much of the city's late 19th century architecture.

Hotel Phillips

106 West 12th Street
1929-1931

Architect:
Boillot & Lauck

Built during the early years of the Great Depression, Hotel Phillips features a brick face intermittently decorated with buff-colored terra cotta tiles and sculptural ornamentation. These Jacobethan Revival elements contrast sharply with the Art Deco style that dominated area construction during the period. The first floor's brown marble transitions into terra cotta facing that extends through the mezzanine's ornate sculptural entablature. Floors four through twenty alternate red brick and terra cotta facing, and the terra cotta sections create a pilaster effect crowned by decorative arches above the 20th floor.

The Hotel Phillips is also an excellent example of historic preservation. Originally built to serve the convention trade, the luxurious Phillips was once the tallest hotel in Kansas City, and did a brisk business before closing in the 1970s. Placed on the National Register in 1979, the Phillips was transformed into a boutique hotel after an extensive remodel in the early 2000s.

Muehlebach Hotel

1204 Baltimore Avenue
1914-1915

Architect:
Holabird & Roche, Chicago

Builder:
Westlake Construction Co.

The Muehlebach Hotel formally opened in May 1915. For many years the hotel was owned by the Truman Hotel Co. and was managed by hotel entrepreneur Barney Allis. Through history the hotel has played host to many renowned personalities and was once called the "temporary White House of President Harry Truman."

The building expresses an adaptation of Beaux-Arts Classicism in its paired pilasters of the upper stories, the repetitive cornices, and the use of classical ornament in the medallions and swags across the facade. The arched ground floor windows are now covered with canopies. Fenestration primarily consists of individual, one-over-one windows with jack arches. The building has recessed entries on the east and north facades. In 1952 the building was expanded to the west with an eleven-story addition.

Midland Office and Theater Building

1221 Baltimore Avenue & 1228 Main Street
1926-27

Architect:
Thomas Lamb, New York
Boller Brothers, Kansas City

Builder:
Boaz-Kiel Construction Co.,
St. Louis

This magnificent steel frame and masonry complex is an exemplary monument to the opulence of the 1920s. The complex consists of a 12-story office building adjoined to a six-story theater structure containing some of the city's most lavish interiors. Designed in a Second Renaissance Revival style, the complex contains a varied array of architectural influences, ranging from the French Baroque and Austrian Rococo to the Commercial style of the 20th century. Of note are the ornate terra cotta embellishments and the grand, arcaded loggia along the 13th Street facade. The complex had its gala opening in 1927.

Municipal Auditorium

211 West 13th Street
1933-1934

Architects:
Gentry, Voscamp & Neville
Hoit, Price & Barnes

This monumental structure is a dramatic example of Art Deco design, and was constructed during the Great Depression at a cost of $6.5 million. The limestone exterior, over huge amounts of steel and concrete, displays a strong massing. The stark exterior is relieved by bold linear motifs and stylized medallions portraying the intellectual and social purpose for which the building is used. Of additional note is the use of side concourses for the movement of large crowds. The structure contains various assembly spaces including an Arena, Music Hall, Little Theater, Exhibition Hall, and committee rooms.

Kansas City Power & Light Bldg.   **44**

1330 Baltimore Avenue
1930-1931

Architect:
Hoit, Price & Barnes

Builders:
Swenson Construction Co.
Long Construction Co.

Upon its completion, the Kansas City Power and Light Building became the tallest building in the State of Missouri. This limestone faced, steel frame structure has 30 floors crowned by a finial shaft equivalent in height to six additional stories. The building, utilizing stepbacks typical of High Rise architecture of the 1930s, is a masterpiece of Art Deco design. An important element in the building's design is the exterior lighting. Each recessed step conceals flood lights, and the crowning shaft features prismatic glass panels and alternating multicolored lights.

The President Hotel

45

1329 Baltimore Avenue
1925

Architect:
Shepard & Wiser

Builder:
George Siedhoff

A project of the Westport Hotel Operating, Co., this 453 room hotel was built at a cost of 2.5 million and featured a rooftop garden that could seat 650. In 1928, it was the headquarters for the Republican National Convention, which nominated Herbert Hoover for president. The hotel's famous Drum Room lounge attracted entertainers including Frank Sinatra and Benny Goodman.

This 15-story Tudor Revival hotel has many decorative details, including a terra cotta cornice string course above the 12th story and pedimented window surrounds surmounted by an intermittent balustrade and quatrefoils. The east wall is pierced by a light court with a gable roof at its base and a bridge at the upper floors that connects the two wings. The hotel underwent a 45.5 million dollar rehab in 2005 after being closed for 25 years.

Mainstreet Theater

1400 Main St.
1921

Architect:
C.W. & George L. Rapp,
Chicago

Builder:
Thompson-Starrett
Construction Co.

A striking example of Beaux Arts style, the Mainstreet Theater is a visual reminder of the movie's golden age. Designed by Rapp and Rapp, a prominent Chicago architectural firm, the four-story theater's dominant feature is its terra cotta-tiled Byzantine styled dome. Other classical embellishments include: trumpet and harp themed frieze, Ionic cornice, and pilasters separating the bays. The main auditorium block is set back from the façade, constructed of buff brick, and features a green-tiled roof.

The theater closed and reopened under different names several times from 1938-1985, as each new ownership group tried various schemes to make the massive theater viable, including subdividing it into several different theatres. Closing in 1985, the theater remained dormant until reopening in 2009.

Jenkins Music Co. Building

1217 Walnut Street
1912; add.1932; alt. 1985

Architects:
Smith, Rea & Lovitt
Charles A. Smith; HNTB

Builder:
Harvey Stiver, R.J. Rector

This building was constructed in two phases for the J. W. Jenkins Sons Music Company, founded in 1878 and originally located at 615 Main Street. A six-story north building was erected in 1912, and in 1932, the south half of the building was constructed with two floors added atop the 1912 unit. The linear Art Deco terra cotta creates a dramatic vertical effect on the unaltered west facade.

Only the facade and first bay remain after the construction of the parking garage.

Bonfils Building

1200 Grand Avenue
1925

Architect:
Frederick C. Gunn

Builder:
Swenson Construction Co.

This two-story masonry and steel building was named for Frederick G. Bonfils, publisher of the Kansas City Post from 1909 to 1922. The elaborate use of Venetian Renaissance Revival style elements reflects the flamboyance of Kansas City life in the 1920s.

Boley Clothing Co. Building

1130 Walnut Street
1909

Architect:
Louis S. Curtiss

"Light and plenty of it," was stressed by Curtiss during the planning of this building, considered his most important work. This six-story, steel and reinforced concrete structure with Art Nouveau elements is significant as one of the earliest major metal and glass curtain-wall buildings in the world.

Bryant Building

1100 Grand Boulevard
1929-1931

Architect:
Frederick E. McIlvain

Builder:
Thompson-Starrett
Construction Co.

A quintessential Art Deco skyscraper, the 26-story steel-framed Bryant Building was completed in 1931. The office building's first three floors are faced with granite ashlar; terra cotta and cream-colored brick cover the rest of the facade, which accentuates the Bryant's dominant vertical lines, and a host of Art Deco inspired reliefs, fluting, floral designs, and brass door enframements maintain the clean lines that characterized Art Deco design.

The Bryant Building's setbacks met the requirements of the city's 1923 Zoning Ordinance, which mandated setbacks as a means to ensure that adequate light and air moved through the congested downtown core.

Curtiss Studio Building

1118-1120 McGee Street
1909-1909

Architect:
Louis S. Curtiss

The structural design genius of Curtiss is exemplified in this three-story building and the abutting commercial building at 1114 McGee Street erected in 1904. Both are early examples of glass curtain-wall design. The Empress Theater, now demolished, was built directly south of the Studio Building. Curtiss secretly opened a passageway, leading to his private theater box, between the two buildings.

Federal Reserve Bank

925 Grand Boulevard
1920, 1986 rehab.

Architect:
Graham, Anderson, Probst &
White, Chicago

Builder:
George Fuller Construction
Co.

This 21-story Classical Revival high-rise housed the Federal Reserve Bank's 10th District operations from its completion in 1921 until 2008. The U-shaped building pairs a steel structure faced with Bedford limestone. The façade design features a three-story base, a thirteen-story shaft, and a five-story cap. Columns denote the main (west) entrance, matching pilasters adorn the adjacent northern and southern facades, and intricate relief work depicting classical inspired American iconography decorates the base.

The building's Neoclassical style reflects popular trends in early 20th century architecture while also matching the building's purpose.

R.A. Long Building

928 Grand Boulevard
1906

Architect:
Howe, Hoit & Cutler

Builder:
C. Everett Clark Co., Chicago

A testament to the Long-Bell Lumber Company's late-19th century success, the R.A. Long Building is also notable as the first steel-frame commercial high-rise office building in downtown Kansas City. Long desired a building that would reflect not only his companies' success, but also contribute to Kansas City's conscious efforts to match commercial utility with civic beauty.

Long turned to the noted architect Henry Hoit to realize his vision. Hoit paired a steel frame with a three-part Italian Renaissance façade to deliver a design that coupled innovative infrastructure with Neoclassical design. The base features red and white granite-clad pilasters; the midsection is clad in gray brick, and an elaborate carved stone entablature crowns the ornate two-story cap.

Long was pleased with Hoit's aesthetic, and even chose Hoit for his eternal needs – the architect designed Long's mausoleum in Forrest Hill Cemetery.

National Bank of Commerce Building

54

922 Walnut Street
1908

Architect:
Jarvis Hunt

Builder:
G. A. Fuller Construction Co.

Several prominent Kansas City bankers, including Dr. W. S. Woods and William Thornton Kemper, Sr., launched the Commerce Trust Company in 1906. Anticipating continued financial growth in the region, Woods ordered a grand skyscraper design from Chicago architect Jarvis Hunt. The proposed building would house the newly founded Commerce Trust Company as well as Woods' pre-existing financial institution, the National Bank of Commerce. The building opened in 1908, forever altering the skyline by initiating Kansas City into the age of the skyscraper, as well as linking Kansas City to influential international architectural design trends that trace their lineage back through Chicago to the École des Beaux-Arts style. The building's design mimics a column: red granite base, stone shaft, and ornate capital. The Commerce Trust met the square-footage needs of booming early 20th century commerce, while stylistically adhering to the conservative ideals of Beaux Arts Neoclassical design.

Fidelity National Bank & Trust

909 Walnut Street
1930-1931

Architect:
Hoit, Price & Barnes

Builder:
Thompson-Starrett
Construction Co.

An exemplary Art Deco high rise, the Fidelity National Bank and Trust Building has undergone radical changes in purpose since its construction. The company, founded in 1899, was a major force in the thriving Kansas City banking community. Fidelity's rapid growth lead to a workforce dispersed throughout the sprawling Kansas City metro, and the bank decided to consolidate its efforts under one roof. The architects created a modern brick and terra cotta clad Art Deco design with a series of characteristic setbacks (above the base and at the 26th and 31st floors). With its distinctive twin-tower crown, the Fidelity Trust joined a booming cohort of Art Deco-inspired buildings downtown.

The economic stresses of the Great Depression proved too much - the bank failed and was liquidated within a year of moving into the new building. The federal government acquired the building during the Truman administration, and renamed it the Federal Office Building. After four decades of occupancy, the federal government "quit" the building in the mid-1990s. Developers acquired the property in 2000 and converted it for use as condominiums.

Gumbel Building

801 Walnut Street
1904

Architect:
John W. McKecknie

This six-story building is the first sizeable building of reinforced concrete in Kansas City. Reinforced concrete construction enabled McKecknie to utilize the tripartite windows, known as "Chicago Style Windows." These permitted more natural light into the interiors of the building.

Scarritt Building

818 Grand Boulevard
1906-1907

Architect:
Root & Siemens

The Scarritt Building and Arcade show the strong influence of the Chicago School of Architecture and, in particular, of the architect Louis Sullivan. The 11-story Scarritt Building consists of a steel skeletal frame, sheathed in brick with rich terra cotta embellishments and has a

Scarritt Arcade

Scarritt Arcade
819 Walnut Street
1907

Architect:
Root & Siemens

similar entry detail to the Arcade. The Scarritt Arcade, facing west on Walnut Street, is a four-story steel frame structure adjoining the Scarritt Building.

Federal Courthouse

811 Grand Boulevard
1938-1939

Architect:
Wight & Wight

Builder:
Swenson Construction Co.

The 1930s were a busy decade for the Kansas City
architectural firm of Wight & Wight. They designed the
Jackson County Courthouse (1934), City Hall (1937),
and the Municipal Courts Building (1938) along with
the Federal Court House, which displays art moderne
sensibilities with distinctive Art Deco flourishes, such as
the intricate brass grillwork covering the three main entry
bays, and the decorative geometric spandrel panels. The
base is faced in granite and the tower is covered with
smooth limestone veneer. The building made headlines
with its air-conditioning system, a necessity by modern
standards but a futuristic luxury in 1939. Notable cases
tried at the court include Kansas City, Mo. v. Williams,
where the federal court affirmed a lower court ruling
desegregating Swope Park Pool. Future Supreme Court
Justice Thurgood Marshall was part of a legal team that
represented the plaintiffs.

Pickwick Hotel, Office Building, Parking Garage & Bus Terminal

60

901-931 McGee Street
1929-1930

Architect:
Wight & Wight

Builder:
Thompson-Starrett
Construction Co.

The Pickwick Hotel Complex contains an 11-story hotel, parking garage, six-story office building, and the massive Union Bus Terminal. Designed by the local firm Wight & Wight, the complex has brick veneers, cut stone piers, caps, and parapets atop a reinforced concrete and steel frame structure. The design evokes Art Deco and Classical elements that would typify Wight & Wight's later work.

Beyond its architectural significance, the Pickwick complex has a historical connection to one of Kansas City's most noted native sons, Harry Truman. A frequent guest from 1930-34, Truman would journal on hotel stationery, detailing the ethical dilemmas endemic to Jackson County political life and contemplate a run for U.S. Senate in 1934. Commonly known as Truman's "Pickwick Papers," these candid manuscripts are available at his presidential library in Independence, Mo.

Stine & McClure Undertaking Co.   **61**

924 Oak Street
1912

Architect:
John W. McKecknie

Appearing dwarfed between the taller adjoining structures, this building of reinforced concrete, cut stone and
terra cotta is a fine example of 20th century Egyptian
Revival style. It was built as an undertaking establishment for Edward Stine, who, in 1860, founded the firm
now known as Stine & McClure.

Public Library Building

62

500 East 9th Street
1895-1897; add. 1917-1918

Architects:
W.F. Hackney & Adriance Van Brunt
Charles A. Smith (north add.)

Developer:
Board of Education

A symbol of the growing intellectual and cultural con-
sciousness of 19th century Kansas City, the library
served as a repository for books and also housed an art
and a science collection. It is designed in the Second
Renaissance Revival style. The building's rich classical
detail is enhanced by a frieze that bears the names of
distinguished Americans, primarily 19th century authors
and statesmen.

The art collection and the scientific collection later developed into two of the city's most outstanding institutions:
the Nelson-Atkins Gallery of Fine Art and the Kansas
City Museum of History and Science.

St. Patrick Church

800 Cherry Street
1875-1881

Architect:
Asa Beebe Cross (attrib.)

Builders:
D. Underwood, brickwork; M. Dunlap, stone cutting;
L.G. McGillis, carpentry

St. Patrick Parish was established in 1869 to serve the increasing number of Catholic families – mostly Irish – who were settling east of Main Street following the Civil War. Ground was broken in May 1875. Parishioners made the bricks, did the bricklaying and held festivals to raise money to erect this Italianate Revival style church. The church was designed by one of Kansas City's pioneer architects, Asa Beebe Cross, who, in addition to this church, also designed the Old Union Depot and the Gillis Opera House. The church wasn't fully completed until May 1881, though it held the first Christmas mass in 1875. There was a rectory to the south that was demolished in 1982.

St. Mary's Episcopal Church

64

1307 Holmes Street
1887-1888

Architect:
William Hasley Wood

Builder:
Remick & Stone

Not until fifty years after its construction was this red brick English Revival style church consecrated and recognized as "the mother parish of Kansas City." The high altar, made in Italy and decorated by the endolithic process of painting on marble (now regarded as a lost art) is considered by many its most outstanding feature and work of art. In this process, the marble was heated to allow the applied colors to be absorbed through the whole thickness. St. Mary's has survived the changes of its surrounding neighborhood, once a fine residential area.

Jackson County Courthouse

65

415 East 12th Street
1934

Architects:
Wight & Wight,
Keene & Simpson,
Frederick C. Gunn

Builder:
Swenson Construction
Co.

This is the third Jackson County courthouse to be built
in Kansas City. The first two were located in the City
Market area, north of downtown. Presiding Judge Harry
S. Truman was influential in the design, having it based
on a courthouse in Shreveport, Louisiana. Wight and
Wight designed the building in the Art Deco style, and
this would influence the surrounding government buildings constructed during Kansas City's Ten-Year Plan.
Sculptural panels depicting the figures of law and justice
are located just below the first setback and are the works
of Jorgen Dreyer. Hare and Hare were the landscape architects for the project. Truman dedicated the $225,000
building in December 1934.

City Hall

66

414 East 12th Street
1936-1937

Architect:
Wight & Wight

Builder:
Swenson Construction Co.

This distinctive building replaced the previous city
hall located in the City Market in 1937. Wight & Wight
designed this Art Deco skyscraper and many other
government district buildings, including the Jackson
County Courthouse, the Police Station, and the old Federal Courthouse on Grand. At a cost of $8 million, this
29-story skyscraper constructed with 7,800 tons of stone
and 6,800 tons of structural steel expands in the summer making the building almost three inches taller. The
south plaza sits atop a 150-car parking garage and has
distinctive sea horse fountains designed by Carl Paul
Jennewein. Friezes depicting the history of Kansas City
surround the sixth floor.

William B. Floyd Residence   **67**

1633 Madison Avenue
c. 1881

This picturesque brick house with its three-sided mansard roofed bay was built for William B. Floyd, an accounting clerk with the Kansas City, Fort Scott and Gulf Railroad. Like many of his neighbors in the area, Floyd was attracted to the city by the opportunities provided by the railroads and the opening of the Hannibal Bridge across the Missouri River.

J.L. Chapman Residence

1614 Summit Street

1880

Builder:
J. L. Chapman (attrib.)

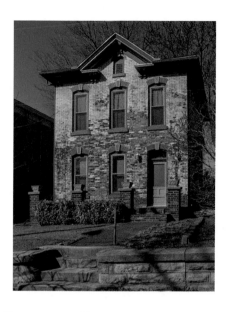

The J. L. Chapman residence is an excellent example of an indigenous architectural form, the Kansas City Peak style. The Peak style was a variation on a more common Italianate design. Typically featuring a three-bay design, the style derived its name from the central gable roof seen above. A small arched window usually adorned the principal street face. This example of the Peak design also features a boxed cornice with coupled brackets and arched lintels with elaborately etched keystones. The original porch was removed but the rest of the structure remains intact. Like the Kansas City Shirtwaist – another local vernacular style – the Peak was popular in Kansas City but was largely unknown elsewhere. Though examples exist in many older neighborhoods throughout the city, the West Side Neighborhood contains the greatest concentration of Peak buildings in Kansas City.

C.H. Townsend Residence 69

1617 Summit Street
c. 1882

Builder:
C.H. Townsend (attrib.)

Built in the 1880s, this two-story house is an example of
the Kansas City Peak style. In 1883, it was the residence
of Charles H. Townsend, a carpenter, who may have
built it. Typical of the style, the house is three bays wide
with a porch across the front and an arched window in its
attic gable. The gable cornice is undecorated, but those
flanking it have elaborate rectangular panels between
pairs of scroll brackets. The handsome porch is original and is distinguished by gear-shaped brackets and
square posts.

John M. Byrne Residence

1745 Summit Street
1899

This two-and-one-half-story red brick Queen Anne house of eleven rooms was built for John M. Byrne, a wealthy lumber dealer. It was an elaborate and expensive residence, as can be seen by the brickwork of the chimneys, the fish scale shingles of the gables, and the multi-paned windows. The Byrne family occupied the house for more than twenty years, at which time they built an even more expensive dwelling in the fashionable Janssen Place.

West High School - Switzer School

1800-2000 Madison Avenue & Summit Street
1899; adds. 1926, 1939, 195, 1958

The Switzer School Buildings consist of five brick educational buildings ranging from two to four stories in height and designed in various architectural styles:

- Switzer School, 1829 Madison, Italian Renaissance Revival style by Charles A. Smith
- West Side Jr. High, 1838 Summit, designed with classical affinities by Charles A. Smith
- Switzer School addition, a PWA Art Deco building affiliated with architect N.W. Downes
- West Side Jr. High Industrial Arts Addition, 20th & Madison, designed in the Constructivist tradition by Curtis & Cowling and constructed in 1956
- Switzer School Primary Unit, 900 W. 18th Street, a Constructivist design by Peterson & Mantel Architects

Switzer School is located in the historic West Side neighborhood that was originally home to a large Swedish, German and Irish population. Today the West Side is the home to a large Hispanic community, mainly housed in mid-to-late 19th and early 20th century single and multi-family residences.

Southwest Tabernacle Congregational Church - West Side Christian Church

700 West Pennway
1888-1889; alt. 1925

This church's construction features load-bearing red brick walls atop a rusticated stone base. The roof is an intersecting gable design, and rounded brick lintels frame its Romanesque arched art-glass windows. The churches' tower connects to the southeastern intersection of the nave and transept, a common characteristic of churches following the vernacular side-steeple layout.

Originally built for the Southwest Tabernacle Congregational Church, the building has changed ownership several times. From 1904-1919 the church was known as the Metropolitan Tabernacle Church. Then, in 1921, the church was sold to the Westside Christian Congregation (Disciples of Christ). A fire destroyed much of the church in 1925, and it was rebuilt with an enlarged auditorium. Since 2000, the building has housed the Rime Buddhist Center, a non-denominational Tibetan Buddhist worship and education center.

First Mexican Baptist Church

801 Avenida Cesar E. Chavez
1945-1946

Architect: Builder:
Albert B. Fuller   C.P. Hucke

This unassuming, Mission style Baptist church features a
double gable roof and a nave and transept cross-shaped
floor plan. Built in 1945 and based on plans by Kansas
City native architect A.B. Fuller, the church was designed
to serve Kansas City's Hispanic community.

Wooden double doors offer entrance from the main,
north facing façade. A door-height stringcourse accents
the entrance. Above the doors, a centrally placed oculus
window sits below a parapet adorned with a Celtic cross.
Three bays of 12-over-16 windows run the length of the
nave, and another three bays of the same windows run
the length of the transept. The church's windows mirror
the bays on the transept, but there are double window
fenestrations in each bay under the nave. A blue, metal-
walled addition connects to the rear of the church.

Evangelical Lutheran Immanuel Church - Our Lady of Guadalupe Shrine

901 Avenida Cesar E. Chavez
1900-1913

Architect:
Van Brunt & Howe

Clad in rusticated stone, this early 20th century Gothic Revival Church was originally built to serve the local Swedish Lutheran community. Instead, it has spent the vast majority of its life as a Catholic parish church. The cornerstone was laid in 1900, and the superstructure was completed in 1913. The Catholic Church purchased the church in 1918, and was renamed Our Lady of Guadalupe Shrine. The church celebrated Catholic mass for the first time on October 5, 1919, and has served the local Hispanic community since that time.

The main façade features a central louvered belfry. Large wooden double doors are crowned with a stained glass pointed arch transom. A rose window occupies the space between the double doors and the belfry. Five bays of stained glass windows run the length of the nave, each bay separated by stone buttresses.

Guadalupe Center

1015 Avenida Cesar E. Chavez
1936

Architect:
Raney & Corman

Builder:
Frank H. Pavlick

Guadalupe Center was established in 1919 to serve
Mexican immigrants. It was organized and staffed by lay
Catholic volunteers who had become aware of the economic exploitation and social discrimination to which the
Mexican community was subjected. The volunteers operated out of several cottages on 23rd Street that in 1935
were demolished to make way for the present facility.
This building, designed primarily by Robert Raney, the
architect for many Fred Harvey system facilities throughout the Southwest, was erected at a cost of $21,000,
with funds donated by Dorothy Gallagher, a longtime
volunteer worker at the center, and her family,

This Pueblo style building, reflecting features of the
Spanish, Mexican and Indian architecture of the Southwest, continues to provide social services for all residents of the area regardless of ethnicity.

Fire Station No. 9

919 West 24th Street
1904

Architect:
John W. McKecknie

Known as Hose Company No. 9, this station was one of many built during the boom years of the 1880s. This station was built during the tenure of the city's most illustrious fire chief, George C. Hale, a strict disciplinarian who inaugurated twice daily drills. According to a 1900 "Record of Quick Hitching," Hose Company No. 9 could hitch in three seconds, if men and horses were on the same floor. Hale's fire department became internationally famous when it was twice selected to represent the United States at the International Fire Congress of London in 1893 and of Paris in 1900.

Sacred Heart Catholic Church

2540 Madison Avenue
1896-1897

Architect:
Gunn & Curtiss (attrib.)

Between 1880 and 1905, 14 Catholic parishes were established in Kansas City, including this one at 26th Street and Madison Avenue. It was founded in 1887 to serve the largely Irish population of the neighborhood. The first pastor was the Rev. Michael J. O'Dwyer, an immigrant from County Limerick in Ireland. At first, services were held in the homes of the parishioners. Later a temporary structure was erected. In 1896 the present Neo-Romanesque style edifice was built, with the pastor and parishioners supplying much of the labor. The turret-topped campanile with its horseshoe arches is particularly notable.

Holy Rosary Catholic Church

911 East Missouri Avenue
1903

The north side and its Italian community have found the
Holy Rosary Catholic Church a steadying influence. The
building itself has been through three fires. On Easter
morning in 1903, a fire that started in the Campbell
Street Methodist Church next door spread to the Holy
Rosary Church, leaving only the rock basement. There
was another fire in 1948 that destroyed the interior, and
in 1955 a fire destroyed the altar. Holy Rosary and the
Don Bosco Community Center (across the street) still
remain the center of neighborhood activity.

R. Nigro & Brothers Drugstore

520 Campbell Street
1898

Builder:
M. Nigro

This building housed the neighborhood drugstore owned and operated by a prominent family in the Italian community. The store was operated by Michael and Rosa Nigro and their family for more than 75 years. The first-story cast-iron front, providing the support for the brick second story, was an innovative 19th century concept allowing the use of large glass display windows.

Apartment Houses

513-519 Harrison Street

Porches are an architectural keynote in the area known as "Little Italy." They are generally later additions to apartments constructed at the turn of the century, when this was a residential area of a burgeoning city.

Antonio Affronti Building & Apartments

517 Gillis Street
1907-1908

Builder:
Issachar J. Dando

These three-story apartments typify early 20th century domestic design. This building with its later side porches was built for Antonio Affronti, a grocer. His store occupied the first floor, with living quarters above.

Garrison Community Center

1124 East 5th Street
1913

Architect:
Ben J. Lubschez of Adriance Van Brunt & Co.

Builder:
George H. Seidoff Construction Co.

Since its opening, this handsome building containing a gymnasium, assembly hall, and library has served the social needs of the neighborhood. The brown and buff colored brick with white stone trim illustrates the tapestry brick design.

Heim Fire Station No. 20

2701 Guinotte Avenue
1903

Owned by the city, privately operated by the Heim Brewery Company, and known as Heim No. 20, this red brick, one-bay station provided fire protection for the East Bottoms.

Heim Brewery Bottling Plant

501 North Montgall Avenue
1903

Architect:
Charles A. Smith

Builder:
Hucke & Sexton

The Heim Brewery sprang to life in 1887 when Ferdinand Heim and his three sons purchased 10 acres that included a factory. They soon erected a huge malt house and transformed the old factory into dry cellars. The imposing two-story red and buff brick building was part of the brewery complex. The Heim family came to Kansas City from East St. Louis in 1884.

Eighth Street Residences

1100-1110 8th Street
1895

Developer:
W. D. Oldham

These six, two-and-one-half-story brick residences in downtown Kansas City form one of the last remaining rows of builder houses. Alternating stylistic details such as the Palladian windows in three of the attic level gables give variety to the six houses. They were erected by W.D. Oldham, a wealthy wholesale grocer with an interest in real estate.

First Church of Christ, Scientist   86

1117 9th Street
1897; 1909

Architects: Builder:
George Mathews   Wilson & Lonsdale
Edwards & Sunderland (1909)

Christian Science spread across the nation with great
speed at the end of the 19th century. This church was
built in 1898, less than twenty years after Mary Baker
Eddy founded the religion. In 1881, Eddy created the
Massachusetts Metaphysical College to educate students interested in Christian Science; one of her early
students, Emma Behan, was responsible for founding Christian Science in Kansas City. Behan opened
an office in Kansas City in 1886. A little more than a
decade later, the First Church of Christ, Scientist, was
erected in Kansas City. With rusticated ashlar stone
and Gothic style, the church exemplifies revival-inspired
architectural trends. The structure's red terra cotta roof
contrasts with the gray stone construction. Large glass
windows decorate the nave, supported by stone tracery
in a recurring Gothic arched motif. Rose windows adorn
the church's various gable ends, and crenelated dormer
windows accentuate the nave's north facing roof.

Masonic Temple

903 Harrison Street
1909-1911

Architect:
James C. Sunderland

Builder:
Birney A. Bowmaster

The Masonic Temple is a fine example the Classical Revival characteristic of the Beaux Arts style. The Temple was constructed with a structural steelframe, reinforced concrete subfloors, and features brick walls with Missouri limestone embellishments, including fluted limestone pilasters on the primary western façade. The third story windows are framed with delicate banderol molding, while windows on the first and second story are each adorned with stone corbels. A cartouche, bearing the Mason's Square and Compass logo, adorns the lintel above the main entry doors.

The Temple was the collaborative project of several local Kansas City Masonic groups. The first Masonic lodges in the Kansas City region were organized in 1848. By 1911, Kansas City had ten lodges. Fire destroyed their previously rented meeting space, and led the various groups to pool their resources and construct this temple for exclusive Masonic use.

Woodland Avenue to Montgall Avenue
St. John Avenue to Independence Avenue

Noted for its architecture and distinct ethnic character, the Pendleton Heights District borders Columbus Park to the west and the Scarritt Point District to the east. Substantially established by 1900, the neighborhood features a mixture of both prominent homes and modest housing. Independence Boulevard, the neighborhood's southern border, was the site of grand construction during the late 19th century. Later developments, including brick apartments and frame homes, joined the pre-existing stately homes and increased the district's architectural diversity. The district notably contains the largest concentration of Queen Anne style properties in Kansas City.

Kansas City was home to a sizable foreign-born Italian immigrant community. Mid-20th century freeway and housing project construction created a physical divide in a previously unified ethnic area. In spite of these barriers, the Pendleton Heights District maintains a discernible architectural and ethnic significance.

Phillip E. Chapell Residence

1836 Pendleton Avenue

1888

Architect:
Harry Kemp

Builder:
T. Howard Oliver

The graceful embodiment of the Queen Anne style is seen in this house built for Philip E. Chapell, ex-treasurer of the State of Missouri and vice president of the Citizen's National Bank. The builder, Oliver, came to Kansas City from St. Louis in 1884 and earned a reputation for quality brick work. He took special pride in this house, using it as an example for subsequent clients. This streetscape typifies a neighborhood built through the sale of a few individual lots for large homes.

Flavel B. Tiffany Residence

100 Garfield Avenue
1908-1909

Architect:
Clifton B. Sloan

Builder:
J.E. Keeler

This dramatic castellated structure known as "Tiffany Castle" was inspired by Dr. Tiffany's European travels and originally was furnished with medieval relics. According to the architect, it was "the first residence in the city to be built of reinforced concrete." Wood was used only for the flooring and interior finish.

Cliff Drive & North Terrace Park (Kessler Park)

1899

Landscape Architect:
George Kessler

Cliff Drive winds along the bluffs overlooking the Missouri River offering views of the river valley from Scarritt Point and Prospect Point. The drive was designed by George E. Kessler, landscape architect, and conducts the motorist through what was originally called North

Terrace Park but now bears Kessler's name. Land for the park was both purchased from and donated by the Scarritt family, beginning in 1899, although plans for its development had been formulated as early as 1893. Part of the roadway was originally a path used by the Scarritt boys to drive cows to Scarritt Spring, which was restored in 1959 by the Board of Park Commissioners. The drive takes advantage of a natural ledge of rocks extending along the side of the bluffs of North Terrace to Scarritt Point where a clean sweep of the river, Clay County, and the East Bottoms is presented.

Scarritt Point District

Named after Nathan Scarritt, a farmer and Methodist minister who bought most of the land during the tumultuous Civil War era, the Scarritt Point District was the product of equal parts affluence and intention. Kansas City's late 19th century industrial and commercial boom brought great wealth, and at the same time, a band of elite citizens conscientiously advocated for Kansas City to follow the City Beautiful plan. The Board of Park Commissioners and noted landscape architect George E. Kessler advocated for the plan, which called for a series of large parks connected by a network of grand boulevards, ensuring that Kansas City would become a cosmopolitan metropolis.

Centered on North Terrace Park, the Scarritt Point District became the destination address for affluent Kansas Citians. Its open spaces offered opportunities for the wealthy to construct luxurious homes. These new parkside abodes dwarfed Quality Hill, the city's formerly most desirable address, which had declined in prestige due to encroachment from nearby industrial and commercial districts. Scarritt Point's residential structures represent the diverse trends in high-end architecture. Construction in the district took place predominantly from 1886-1915, and includes fine examples of American Four-Square, Queen Anne, Beaux Arts, Colonial Revival, Mission Revival, and Craftsman styles. Lacking substantial new construction since 1920, the district maintains its vibrant late-Victorian architectural flavor.

William Wallace Residence

3200 Norledge Avenue
1888, 1909

Architect:
Loren Grant Middaugh (1909)

This unique vernacular structure at 3200 Norledge was originally built in a different location and with a distinctly different aesthetic. Constructed for Judge William Hockaday Wallace, a prosecuting attorney for Jackson County, the red brick house stood on what would become the corner of Gladstone Boulevard and Walrond Road. A decade later, R.A. Long, the local lumber magnate, decided to relocate to Scarritt Point. Long selected the Gladstone boulevard location for his mansion, and needing the entire block, entered into an agreement to move the Wallace home a block north to 3200 Norledge.

Long had the red brick Wallace home transformed. The redesigned building features a rusticated limestone wall treatment and newly flattened roof surrounded by a crenelated parapet. What had been a multi-story Queen Anne style red brick home was transformed into something of a Gothic, castle-like structure. A private residence for many years, the new-look Wallace home is now an annex of the Kansas City Museum, which is housed in Long's former mansion, Corinthian Hall.

William Chick Scarritt Residence 94

3240 Norledge
1888

Architect:
John Welborn Root

This brownstone and brick residence was constructed at
a cost of $30,000 for William Chick Scarritt, a member of
one of Kansas City's pioneering and land owning families. The house is an example of the Chateauesque style
adapted from French Gothic and Renaissance chateaux
of the 15th and 16th centuries. Once used as a nursing
home, the residence is distinguished by a three-story
semi-cylindrical bay, convex windows with leaded art
glass transoms, and a recessed main entrance portico.
The scrolled iron grillwork in the round arch entrance
features the cipher of the carver.

R.A. Long Residence - Corinthian Hall

3218 Gladstone Boulevard
1909-1910

Architect:
Henry F. Hoit

Builder:
George W. Huggins

Currently housing the Kansas City Museum, this home was originally built for Robert A. Long, a lumber magnate, civic leader and philanthropist (Long spearheaded and contributed heavily to the Liberty Memorial.) The Long residence is a wealth of classical architectural details, quality construction and exquisite workmanship, and is probably the most notable example of Beaux Arts Classicism in the city. The entire complex achieves harmony through uniformity in its red tile roofs, Bedford limestone facing, and repetition of design elements and details.

The era in which the residence was built was a time of income tax repeal as well as an open-door policy toward immigration which provided the plentiful, cheap labor and skilled craftsmen. The Beaux Arts style was the favored mode for the grandiose house as a public badge of class distinction for men of great wealth. These factors have enabled the R.A. Long residence to become a monument to a by-gone era in Kansas City's architectural history.

Gladstone Boulevard Mansions

On high bluffs overlooking the Missouri River, Kansas Citians erected elegant homes that for about 20 years after the turn of the century served as one of the glittering focuses of Kansas City's social life. Fashionable homes also were built along Armour Boulevard, The Paseo, and Independence Avenue, but only here do so many representative examples survive. Writing in 1881, the author of a "History of Jackson County, Missouri" prophetically described this beautiful site: "Nature has formed and fashioned these grounds especially for the erection of elegant houses where a grand panorama of beauty can be viewed from every doorway."

Mrs. Harvey A. Brower Residence   96

3425 Gladstone Boulevard
1909

Architect:
Frederick H. Michaelis

Judge E.L. Scarritt Residence 97

3500 Gladstone Boulevard
1899

Architect:
Frederick E. Hill

Builder:
Martin E. Tomlinson

Calvert Hunt Residence 98

3616 Gladstone Boulevard
1904

Architect:
John W. McKecknie

Heim Brothers Residences

320-328 Benton Boulevard
1895; 1897 (carriage house)

Architect:
Charles A. Smith

Builder:
Hucke & Sexton

Ferdinand Jr. and Michael Heim were two of the three sons of Ferdinand Heim Sr., an Austrian immigrant who established his Heim Brewery Company in East St. Louis before moving the operation to Kansas City in 1884. The brothers invested in a streetcar, and although it was a flop at first, it quickly became popular after the brothers built The Electric Park amusement park at the end of the streetcar line in 1899.

Ferd and Michael hired the prolific architect Charles Smith to design two homes on the same block of Benton Avenue in the fashionable Northeast neighborhood of the city. Ferd's home, at 320 Benton, was designed in the Victorian Eclectic style while Michael's, at 328 Benton, was designed in the Queen Anne style. Not long after, the two brothers built a long carriage house at the back of the lot between their residences. To get to the buildings, carriages exit the street onto a heart-shaped driveway that loops around a fountain in the center of the properties.

Benton Boulevard Streetscape

300-340 Benton Boulevard

An 1890 map of Kansas City containing the original study for a city park system shows Benton Boulevard, named for Senator Thomas Hart Benton, as the major north-south thoroughfare extending from Linwood Boulevard to North Terrace Park. Boulevards were designed to permit the easy flow of traffic and were landscaped to be visually pleasing. To further enhance the streetscapes, imposing houses were built along the boulevards. Particularly noteworthy as a feature of the boulevard concept are these handsome residences built between 1888 and 1908 on the west side in the 300 block of Benton Boulevard.

Bellefontaine Avenue District

101

502-524 Bellefontaine Avenue
1890

Cut stone, wood trim and stained glass front windows embellish these two-story red brick single family homes, most of which retain the original front porches. These substantial middle-class homes feature stylistic details inspired by the English designer Charles Eastlake. Original owners included a grocer, a civil engineer, an attorney, and Maurice E. Bates, an engineer who helped construct Kansas City's first electric street railway.

Milo E. Lawrence Residence

512 Benton Boulevard
1888

This exotic Queen Anne style residence is of cut stone, slate shingle, and cast iron. The exterior is distinguished by a sculpture of an Assyrian mythological figure utilized as the porch post, a carved bust of a woman in the porch entrance, and the body of a dragon more than 20 feet long on the front wall. Though owned by three different people during its construction, Milo E. Lawrence, secretary and manager of the Standard Fire Insurance Company, is believed to have been the first owner to have occupied the house.

Independence Boulevard Christian Church

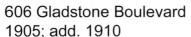

606 Gladstone Boulevard
1905; add. 1910

Architect:
Howe, Hoit & Cutler

Builder:
Hollinger & Mitchell

Independence Boulevard Christian Church is a two-story Neoclassical Disciples of Christ church. With its striking Ionic columns and large domed nave, the church could easily be mistaken for a courthouse or other secular structure. The church was originally founded as an affiliate of the First Christian Church, a Disciples Church located in downtown Kansas City. Churchgoers from Kansas City's growing Northeastern neighborhoods sought a place of worship near their homes. The first Disciples church in the Northeast was built at Sixth and Prospect in 1890. In 1891, local lumber magnate and influential Kansas Citian R.A. Long joined the congregation.

Long's membership forever altered the church's fortunes. Long purchased land on Independence Boulevard and Gladstone, and spearheaded the construction of the church building seen above. Completed in 1905, the church was initially symmetrical, but Long would eventually fund the western addition in 1909 and the carillon bell tower in 1919. The 1909 addition was particularly notable as it included an education building, gymnasium, and swimming pool.

Lutheran Church
of Our Redeemer

711 Benton Boulevard
1922

The Lutheran Church of Our Redeemer congregation
was organized in January 1922. The first chapel was
dedicated in May 1922, the first parish hall dates from
1923, and the original chapel was enlarged in 1931.
Built of stucco and wood in the Tudor Revival style, the
church's main façade is white with dark brown half-timbers. The main entrance, a pair of wooden double doors,
is accessible from the western main façade. The gable
roof porch mimics the steep gable roof of the nave.
Paired, narrow rectangular art glass windows adorn
either side of the front façade, and the windows continue
in symmetrical bays down the nave towards the transept.
Concrete buttresses separate the window bays. The
transept ends terminate in an entrance way covered by a
gabled roof.

Oakley Methodist Episcopal Church

4600 East Independence Avenue
1902-1903

Architect:
Shepard & Farrar

Built of local native stone quarried in what would become Kessler Park, and designed by the local architectural firm Shepard & Farrar, the Oakley United Methodist Church is made of Kansas City materials. The design leans heavily on Gothic revival style, with its rusticated stone walls, lancet arches, and the crenelated parapet that surrounds the tower and chancel. Three stone buttresses separate art glass window bays, and a large stone chimney rises from the nave's eastern gable end. Sets of decorative art windows, set in stone tracery, adorn the semi-hexagonal apse on the church's western end. Originally serving an English-speaking congregation, the church has been renamed Camino Verdad y Vida United Methodist Church. It now offers Spanish language services, a change that reflects the shifting ethnic population in historic Northeast Kansas City.

Northeast High School

415 Van Brunt Boulevard
1912

Architect: Builder:
Smith, Rea & Lovitt   Charles W. Lovitt

Charles A. Smith designed all but one of the Kansas City school buildings constructed between 1910 and 1918. During this period of new ideas in school building design, Smith designed with expansion in mind. His plans were to be practical rather than extravagant. Designed in the Neoclassical revival style, three-story Doric columns visually supporting a classical pediment mark the entrance bay. Also featured: a terra cotta cornice with dentils, colossal fluted Doric Carthage stone columns, and brick pilasters.

At a cost of $625,000, the building was designed around a large auditorium that could seat 1,600 people. The first-floor plan included a public library branch, vocational training department, auxiliary gymnasium, swimming pool, laundry, kitchen, and cafeteria. The second, third and fourth floors housed a 100 x 60 foot gymnasium, offices, the chemistry and physics departments, zoology and domestic arts classrooms, study halls, a reference library, an emergency room, a model flat, art rooms, and music classrooms.

Montgomery Ward Building 107

6220 St. John Avenue
1913-14; adds. 1925, 1966

Architect:
Frank E. Trask of McKecknie & Trask

Builder:
Wells Brothers Co.

This handsome and innovative reinforced concrete building has been a landmark in the area since its construction. Montgomery Ward made a vital contribution to the
population and economic growth of the northeast by
attracting new residents into the area for jobs, as well as
employing some already residing there.

The "Alligator" House

6405 Independence Avenue
1909

Builder:
William C. Howard

A rustic cottage, deceivingly constructed of concrete with alligators flanking the front steps, came from the imagination of the builder and owner, William C. Howard. The house was remodeled in this manner in 1918 to include the simulation of logs in the upper level.

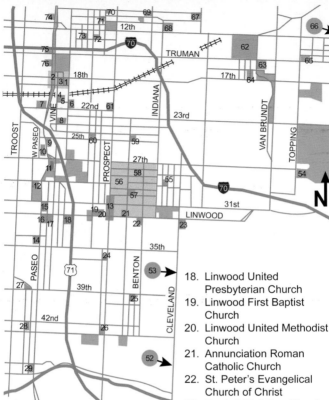

18. Linwood United Presbyterian Church
19. Linwood First Baptist Church
20. Linwood United Methodist Church
21. Annunciation Roman Catholic Church
22. St. Peter's Evangelical Church of Christ
23. Central Christian Church
24. St. Paul's Reformed Presbyterian Church
25. Blessed Sacrament Church
26. Prospect Avenue Presbyterian Church
27. Immanuel Lutheran Church
28. D.W. Newcomer & Sons
29. Victor Beutner Residence
30. Paseo Methodist Church
31. Maud Gray Homes
32. St. George's Parish
33. Philip Rollheiser Residence
34. Boone-Hays Cemetery
35. Benedictine Sanctuary of Perpetual Adoration
36. Forest Hills Cemetery & Pantheon
37. Paseo Christian Church
38. St. John's Seminary
39. Marlborough Area
40. The Paseo Viaducts
41. Ellis Hall (Dodson District)
42. Hare Residences

1. Musician's Union Local 627
2. 18th & Vine District
3. Gem Theater
4. Vine Street Workhouse
5. Fire Station No. 11
6. Lincoln High School
7. Armour Memorial & Gillis Orphans
8. Bethel A.M.E. Church
9. Paseo Baptist Church
10. Robinson Hospital
11. Troost Lake
12. St. George's Parish House
13. Troost & 31st Commercial District
14. Keneseth Israel-Beth Shalom Synagogue
15. St. Vincent de Paul Church
16. St. Dionysios Greek Orthodox Church
17. Temple B'nai Jehudah Synagogue

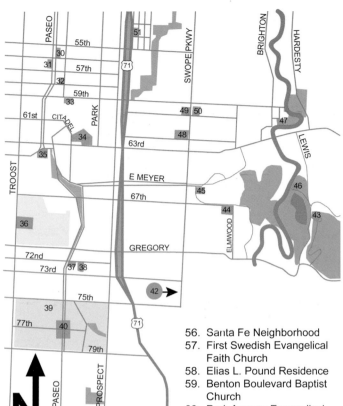

43. Swope Park Memorial and Mausoleum
44. Van Noy Residences
45. Swope Park Shelter House No. 1
46. Swope Park Swimming Pool
47. Byram's Ford
48. Swope Park Christian Church
49. Swope Park Lodge AF & AM No. 617
50. Church of the Covenant
51. Wheatley Public School
52. Robert H. Fitzgerald Residence
53. Fire Station No. 26
54. Santa Fe Trail
55. Church of God, Holiness

56. Santa Fe Neighborhood
57. First Swedish Evangelical Faith Church
58. Elias L. Pound Residence
59. Benton Boulevard Baptist Church
60. Park Avenue Evangelical Church
61. South Prospect Christian Church
62. Elmwood Cemetery
63. St. Paul School of Theology
64. East Kensington Cottages
65. Centropolis Baptist Church
66. St. Stephen Catholic Church
67. Holy Trinity Catholic Church
68. Bales Baptist Church
69. Dorson Apartments
70. Olive Street Baptist Church
71. Central Baptist Church of God in Christ
72. Metropolitan Spiritual Church of Christ
73. Beacon Light Seventh Day Adventist Church
74. Dr. G. L. Henderson Residence
75. St. Stephen Baptist Church
76. St. Monica's Mission Church

East Side
Swope

The East Side and Swope Districts, though separate, share wonderfully rich histories and boast diverse cultural communities, sprawling parks, and boulevards lined with magnificent churches. As the trend to move further south continued, it was evident that the southern reaches of the city would become an integral part of Kansas City. Not far from this southward expansion, the East Side District continued to grow and became a diverse ethnic district.

Spanning from the banks of the Blue River to the Kansas-Missouri State Line and from 47th Street to the south boundary of Jackson County, the South District occupies much of southern Kansas City. In its early history the South District was much like the rest of Kansas City – rolling farmland dotted with country homes. During the late 1800s small communities began to develop such as Waldo at 75th Street and Wornall Road, Dobson at 85th Street and Prospect Avenue, and Dallas at 103rd Street and State Line Road. Though the South District encompasses these small communities as part of Kansas City now, the established communities continue to maintain their separate distinct district (such as Waldo.)

Despite development of communities in the region, much of the district remained rural farmland. Apple orchards largely occupied this rural farmland and provided a perfect location for Kansas City families to picnic and relax. Eventually the farmland gave way to residential development, which accelerated in the 1920s as real estate developers like J.C. Nichols began developing and extending Kansas City's southern limits.

Before southward expansion of the city began and residential communities were constructed, the land awaited a transformation. In the 1890s the transformation of the region began thanks to a donation by Thomas H. Swope, who believed in beautifying the city as far as possible. Swope's vision for the undeveloped land in the South District was realized in a 1,300-acre park that he donated to the city in the 1890s. Initially, the city accepted the donation, but the citizens and city leaders realized funds were not available to maintain the park. The cost of landscaping pastures and woods would exceed the rewards, as well as the fact that the park lay too far out from the city. In 1910, the city annexed the farmland where Swope Park is located and built a boulevard leading to the park. Moreover, development of the area flourished as residential communities sprung up and the city had even begun work on the Kansas City Zoo.

Today Swope Park is an 11-mile expanse of land through which Blue River winds through the center of the park. Following the river, Blue River Parkway is a scenic road that extends from Swope Park southwest to 151st Street and State Line Road. Dotted throughout rolling hillsides and in the shadow of limestone bluffs, small areas of land have been transformed into baseball diamonds and picnic areas. Swope Park is one of the largest parks in the United States, and its scenic roadway (completed in 1973) is evident of the original parks and boulevards plan to follow the natural terrain of the land. It is also an example of Kansas City's timeless philosophy of Daniel Burnham's City Beautiful Movement. Although this movement created vast greenbelts of lush parks and wide boulevards, it simultaneously displaced the impoverished inhabitants of the original boomtown, making it a sometimes controversial city planning tool. Nevertheless, donations such as Thomas H. Swope's allowed for the creation of a wonderful addition to the city that provides a quiet retreat and place for leisurely activities for visitors.

In close conjunction with the South District is the East Side District, which contains a diverse ethnic history. It extends from a concentration of apartments and office buildings on its western boundary of Troost Avenue to a residential area with shopping centers at Kansas City's southeastern city limits of I-435 and Blue Parkway. However, in the 1880s the district was primarily a farming community on the outskirts of Kansas City. An eight-room schoolhouse built in 1897 at 24th Street and Prospect Avenue served the small farming community. The school was designed to serve a widely scattered population but within ten years was expanded to satisfy the concentration of Kansas Citians in the area. By the turn of the century, city officials chose to locate the prison, public works building, and street maintenance buildings along Vine Street in the East Side District.

The East Side District is particularly known for diversity and buildings reflecting distinct cultural and religious groups. Many of the district's building are associated with Kansas City's Jewish community who migrated into the Midwest after the American Civil War. Although a small community existed within Kansas City before 1840, this influx of Jewish immigrants from Germany and Central Europe contributed to the city's population growth as a whole. Early Jewish residents formed their first communal organization, a burial society, in 1864, and later in 1870 established their first synagogue, B'nai Jehudah. A second wave of Jewish immigrants arrived in the 1880s and 1890s from Eastern Europe and settled on the northern edge of the district near Independence and Admiral Boulevards. Here the Jewish community built seven new synagogues.

In addition to the growing number of synagogues, eastern Kansas City included many Catholic and Protestant churches. The majority of these churches lined Linwood Boulevard making Linwood synonymous with "Boulevard of Churches." These churches served Kansas City's English Congregationalist, Scotch Presbyterian, and German and Scandinavian religious communities.

Along with the establishment of Jewish communities in the 1880s, parts of the East Side District were home to African-American communities who concentrated their residences, businesses, and churches in the area north of 28th Street. Due to covenant restrictions, African-Americans were only allowed to live in certain areas of the city. As Jewish immigrants and other ethnic groups moved out of a neighborhood, African-Americans would establish themselves in these areas. During the 1950s the African-American population expanded into the southern part of the East Side District towards The Paseo as well as Troost and Prospect Avenue.

While the East Side District was remembered for its early religious communities and gothic architecture churches, the 18th and Vine District was one of the most unique, historic areas in Kansas City that drew national attention. From 1920 to 1950 this area was the most important business center for the African-American community. Located in a six- to eight-block range within 18th and Vine Streets, the area pulsated with energy, vigor, and commerce. African-American-owned businesses such as hotels, theaters, restaurants, lawyers, dentists, and physicians thrived in the district. The area also included a number of churches as well as NAACP and Urban League offices. One of Kansas City's local newspapers, the Kansas City Call, was established in the area. Yet, despite the overwhelming commercialization of the district, it was the historic jazz community that contributed to the area and city as a whole. During

Prohibition Era, the 18th and Vine District served as the nightlife and entertainment destination because it was the perfect place to hear authentic Kansas City Jazz. On a hot summer night one could hear the sweet sounds of saxophones, pianos, and powerful voices slipping out of the nightclub and into the streets of Kansas City. The jazz district was home to players who would become legends, such as Charlie "Bird" Parker, Count Basie, Big Joe Turner, Bennie Moten, and George and Julia Lee. Today there is an effort to maintain the historic 18th and Vine District by creating a sustainable and economically sound neighborhood that preserves the heritage and legacy of Kansas City's African-American traditions.

Opposite the North end (9th Street) of the East Side District lie suburban residential developments, mostly modest size homes on larger plots of land. In the 1920s construction surged throughout the southern part of the East Side District and includes subdivisions planned by N.W. Dible, one of Kansas City's most prolific homebuilders. It also contains Eastwood Hills, which was built by J.J. Swofford as a country club community. The subdivision was built with the rolling hills and views of downtown as the backdrop for the subdivision. Eastwood Hills is on the edge of the urban core, located in what the city calls the "first ring" suburbs of Kansas City.

Both the South and East Side districts border each other through Swope Parkway. Each contains a vital part of Kansas City History including parks for the City Beautiful Movement and the famous 18th and Vine Jazz District, as well as ethnic diversity and beautifully engineered churches. These districts contribute a rich history to the city that allows Kansas Citians to partake in the diverse ethnicities and cultures within the area.

Musician's Union Local 627

1823 Highland Avenue
1904

Architect:
Rudolf Markgraf

From about 1920 to about 1945, the Kansas City com-
munity thrived on its most famous product – jazz. If any
one place can be said to be the home of the Kansas City
Style, this building would probably be chosen. In 1928
it became the home of the Musician's Union Local 627.
Jazz musicians were drawn to Kansas City during the
Pendergast era, when gambling and night life flourished.
After the demise of that debaucherous period, many jazz
players moved on. The roll of musicians included Charlie
"Bird" Parker, Count Basie, Mary Lou Williams and Baby
Lovett. They helped create the Kansas City Style, which
has been defined this way: "It means a drive, a good
beat, a rhythmic push. It means taking a simple riff and
building up to a moving mass of counterpoint against
the improvisations of the soloists. It means lots of piano,
trumpet and saxophone solos – all ad libbed and without
paper."

18th & Vine District

Bound by covenants and deed restrictions, black Kansas Citians were prohibited from moving south of 27th Street during the first half of the 20th century. As the community grew in population it became completely self-sufficient. Black doctors, dentists, and lawyers practiced and lived in the neighborhood while more than 600 businesses, hotels, theaters, restaurants, and stores flourished.

The 18th & Vine area became the downtown activity center for the black community, surrounded by densely populated neighborhoods. The Kansas City Call newspaper, established in 1919, is one of the country's oldest African-American newspapers and still operates at 1715 East 18th Street.

The area is also well known for the creation of a pioneering style of jazz during the 1920s and '30s, and located nearby was the original baseball stadium for the Negro Leagues' Monarchs.

The Gem Theater

1615-1617 East 18th Street
1912

Architect:
George Carman

Builder:
Patrick J. Morley

The Gem Theater was originally named The Star, and was operated for a period of time by Guy M. Shriner of the Shriner Amusement Company. After its remodeling and renaming in 1924, the theater had a seating capacity of 1,238. The theater was equipped with the (then) most modern of heating, ventilation and projection systems.

The main façade is clad in terra cotta, made especially for the Gem by the Western Terracotta Company. Decorative cartouches and swags surround the windows above the entrance level, and a curvilinear dentil band course defines the cornice area.

Vine Street Workhouse

2001 Vine Street
1897

Architect:
A. Wallace Love

Builder:
Hollinger & Mitchell

Even though it served as a prison, this large and imposing structure of native limestone was seen at the time of
its construction as an "ornament to the city." Prisoners
quarried the stone and helped in the construction.

Across the street at 2000 and 2010 Vine Street are two
Mission style stone public works buildings designed by
S.E. Edwards and constructed in 1906.

Fire Station No. 11

2033 Vine Street
1931

Architect: Builder:
Robin A. Walker;   C.A. Kelly
James O'Connor, consulting architect

Kansas City Fire Department history dates back to 1858, with the formation of the first volunteer fire department. Fire Station No. 11 was first organized in 1890, and it was located in a tent on Independence Avenue between Park and Brooklyn. A new station was built at 1812 Vine Street, in the heart of the 18th & Vine Historic District. This move reflected the growing segregation in the city that relocated African Americans from areas around the city.

In 1931, the city awarded the design contract for a new station to Robin A. Walker, with city architect James O'Connor supervising. The station reflects elements of the Art Deco style, including smooth finish vertical limestone topped with three cusped foil details on either side of the fire engine bay building. The new building featured all of the modern conveniences: hot and cold water, showers, a Frigidaire, lockers with electric lights, a modern hose tower, bunk room, two slide poles and an office.

Lincoln High School

2111 Woodland Avenue
1935; add. 1966-1968

Architect:
Charles A. Smith

Builder:
Swenson Construction Co.

Lincoln High School sits high atop one of the tallest hills on the east side of downtown Kansas City and has an unobstructed view of the central business district. The three-story building was constructed in two phases; the main U-shaped block was completed in 1935, and the hexagonal wings attached to the south end of the original block were added in 1966.

These two distinct construction phases express two very different styles of architecture. The 1935 block is Late Gothic Revival in style, although the abstract and low-relief ornament reflects the influence of the Art Deco aesthetic. The 1966 addition has the geometric form, lack of windows, and simple façade detailing that illustrate the Modern Movement, particularly as it was applied to educational architecture in Kansas City.

Lincoln played a central role in shaping Kansas City's African-American community. As the only high school facility in Kansas City open to African-American students, it continuously promoted the importance of education. Because it was the only secondary school available to them, many of the city's most prominent American-African citizens attended Lincoln.

Gillis Orphan's Home

2119 Tracy Avenue
1899

Architect:
Van Brunt & Howe

Although constructed in different years and designed
by different architects, these two Georgian Revival style
structures functioned as a unit. The Gillis Orphans'
Home and the Armour Home (for the Care of the elderly)
were originally operated by the Women's Christian Association. They are occupied now by the Western Baptist
Bible College, formerly Western Seminary. This school
is said to be "the oldest Christian institution west of the
Mississippi River founded solely for African-Americans."

(Ed. note: Armour Home was demolished in 2016.)

Bethel A.M.E. Church

2329 Flora Avenue
1920-1926

Architect:
Brostrom & Drotts

A large stone tower dominates this crenelated Gothic Revival African Methodist Episcopal church at the corner of Flora and 24th Street. Bethel A.M.E. was designed by two of the most prolific architects of religious buildings in the region, E.O. Bostrom and Phillip Drotts.

Sister Kitty Raynor is said to be the impetus for the church, gathering neighborhood children for Sunday school in her nearby home. A very small group of parishioners first organized the church after purchasing the property in 1920, which included a basement that had already been built by the Second Christian Church. By the time the structure was completed in 1926, the congregation had grown to nearly 700. Prior to the first service on Sunday, September 19, parishioners lined up from Flora to Paseo before marching into their new church while singing "When the Saints Go Marching In."

Paseo Baptist Church

2501 Paseo
1927-1942

Architect:
John H. Felt & Co.

Builder:
G.W. Cope & Sons

This handsome red brick church with cut stone trim has served as a center of worship for the community for 50 years. Organized in 1884 as the Shiloh Baptist Mission at 20th and Main, the Mission eventually relocated to 1825 Vine Street in 1896, and the name was changed to the Vine Street Baptist Church. In 1927, under the leadership of Dr. D. A. Holmes, the church moved to its present location, where it took the name Paseo Baptist Church.

Robinson Hospital

2625 West Paseo Boulevard
1914

Architect:
Henry F. Hoit

Builder:
Hollinger Construction Co.

Robinson Hospital is a rare surviving example of the private hospital buildings constructed prior to World War I in Kansas City. During the early 20th century, different religious and ethnic groups established hospitals for the use of their members. Robinson was the city's only private neurological hospital available for the treatment of the mentally ill beginning in 1935, when Dr. George Wilse Robinson, Sr., one of Kansas City's earliest psychiatrists, was at the forefront of the movement to improve the standards of treatment for addiction and mental disease.

The hospital was designed in Classical Revival style by Kansas City architect Henry F. Hoit. The primary facade is four stories in height with a fifth story that incorporates the central pavilion and recessed conservatories occupying the flat roof of the flanking wings. A pediment roof that caps the central pavilion and the terra cotta ornament of the pavilion further define the Classical Revival style of the building.

Troost Lake

27th Street & Paseo
c. 1889

The land surrounding Troost Lake was originally part of the Rev. James Porter farm. Porter migrated from Nashville with his wife and son in 1832, bringing horses, cattle, hogs, and twenty-five to thirty slaves. At what is now the corner of 27th Street and Tracy Avenue, Porter and his servants constructed Porter's home. For several generations the site was preserved by Porter's descendants.

Eventually the land was bought by the Kansas City Cable Car Company, which opened one of the first amusement parks in Kansas City (in 1889) and called it Troost Park. The park was located at the end of the company's Troost line at 24th Street.

Troost Park was purchased by the city in 1902, but all that remains is the 3-1/2 acre lake. A marker at the southwest end of the lake indicates the site where Joseph Smith and eleven of his followers of the Colesville branch met and camped in August 1831.

St. George's Parish House

2917 Tracy Avenue
1909

Architect:
Howe & Hoit

Builder:
William A. Row

Plans for a grouping of structures for St. George's congregation began in 1909 when it was announced that four buildings – a church, chapel, parish and rectory – would be constructed between 27th and 28th streets at Tracy Avenue. Planned to be erected first were the parish house and rectory. This Gothic style structure, erected in 1909, is all that was actually built. Alterations to the interior were made in 1913.

Troost Avenue was named after Dr. Benoist Troost, an immigrant from Holland. Troost Avenue historically has served as a racial dividing line. The commercial area between 32nd and 34th along Troost began as part of Millionaire's Row – large mansions lined the 3100 block of Troost. As the streetcar lines pushed south on Troost, middle-class housing was developed along with the mansions, and commercial centers developed along Troost to service these new residents. The Isis Theater, Woolworths, Firestone, A&P, the Jones store and J.C. Penney's were some of the businesses located on these blocks that flourished through the early 20th century. With the coming dominance of the automobile cultural and the social upheaval of the '60s and '70s, businesses left and buildings fell into decay.

Keneseth Israel-Beth Shalom Synagogue

3400 Paseo
1926-1927

Architect:
Greenebaum,
Hardy & Schumacher

Builder:
Patti Construction Co.

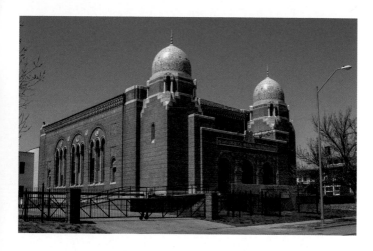

Jewish life in Kansas City goes back to the town's beginnings, possibly as early as the 1830s when partners named Cohn and Block operated a general store. In the 1860s immigrants came primarily from Germany and Western Europe, while in the 1880s, Russian and Eastern European Jews were arriving in large numbers.

In 1908 three Orthodox congregations, including Keneseth Israel, joined to become a single congregation. The building was completed in 1927 at a cost of $400,000. As a Byzantine structure, it features delicately polychromed terra cotta domes.

St. Vincent de Paul Church

3106 Flora Avenue
1922-1932

Architects:
Maurice Carroll, Kansas City, Kansas
& Albert Martin, Los Angeles

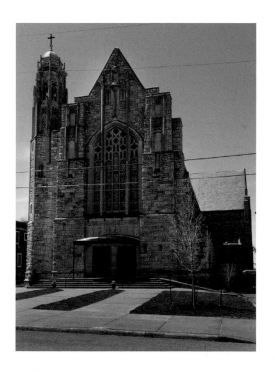

St. Vincent de Paul Church cost $230,000 to build and took 10 years to complete. The object of the design was to build a parish church of Gothic design without copying any existing building. The two transept arches and the main sanctuary arch are all poured monolithic concrete; more than 9,000 sacks of concrete were used during the construction.

Joseph Conradi, a Swiss artist, sculpted the statue of Christ crucified that can be seen on the west elevation.

St. Dionysios
Greek Orthodox Church

1423 East Linwood Boulevard
1938

Architect:
Trevor C. Jones

In 1900, Linwood Boulevard was widened from a regular city street to a 40-foot roadway with 8-foot sidewalks and three rows of trees to shade pedestrians. By 1930, Linwood was known as the Boulevard of Churches, with seven churches, three synagogues, two Masonic temples, the YMHA building, and St. Joseph Hospital. Eight years later, the Greek Orthodox Church of the Annunciation was built at the corner of Linwood and Paseo.

Founded in 1912, the church chose a design in a modern adaptation of Corinthian style. In 1975, the church moved to 12001 Wornall.

Temple B'nai Jehudah Synagogue

 17

1515 East Linwood Boulevard
1908

Architect:
Howe, Hoit & Cutler

Builder:
Taylor & Winn

Congregation B'nai Jehudah was organized in 1870 by 25 Jewish pioneer residents who utilized acreage in Elmwood Cemetery for services until the first permanent sanctuary at 6th and Wyandotte was dedicated in 1875. Two moves later, the congregation settled into this Linwood Boulevard location.

Six fluted Doric columns flank the front entrance, holding up a wide entablature on which rests an unadorned pediment with multiple ornate acroterions. An annex to the rear of the structure, designed by Greenebaum, Hardy & Schumacher, was constructed in 1920.

The congregation expanded and moved yet again in 1956, under the leadership of Rabbi Samuel Mayerberg (1928-1960), an outspoken critic of the Pendergast machine in the 1930s.

Linwood United Presbyterian Church

1801 East Linwood Boulevard
1904, 1909, 1922

Architect:
Frank S. Rea & Charles
Smith (1909)
Greenebaum, Hardy &
Schumacher (1922)

Builder:
Geo. Goodlander (1909)

Construction began in 1904 on this monumental Gothic Revival church, and in 1909 a larger sanctuary and Sunday school rooms were added. Construction on another new sanctuary commenced in 1922, and the church was finally completed in 1923. The building is clad in red brick walls trimmed with beige terra cotta, and a large tower with ornate terra cotta finials dominates the northeast corner of the church.

The dwindling congregation vacated the church in the 1970s. Stained glass, tracery and sanctuary pews were removed, yet the sanctuary retained its balconies, decorative trusses and the organ screen.

Linwood First Baptist Church

2310 East Linwood Boulevard
1909; 1925; 1953

Architect:
Shepard & Farrar (1909)
John H. Felt & Co. (1925)
Edward Tanner (1953)

The property for this church was purchased in 1907 for
$10,000. In 1920, Linwood First Baptist had the larg-
est men's Bible club in the city. By 1925 the church was
enlarged to the east and a $100,000 auditorium was built
around the 1909 section.

A crenelated, 40-foot square tower, projecting entryway
with three portals, art glass windows with tracery and
trefoil designs and windows in pointed arches with cut-
stone pointed-arch drip molds are just a few of the late
Gothic Revival elements found throughout the structure.

Linwood United Methodist Church

2400 East Linwood Boulevard
1904; adds. 1918-1920, 1949-1950

Architect:
Smith, Rea & Lovitt (1918-20)

Builder:
James E. Taylor (1918-20)

Prior to its Linwood location, the Methodist congregation, led by Rev. James Kirk, evolved through several
other locations and names before settling in to a tent on
Olive Street and held their first services there in 1902.
Construction began on the basement in 1903. In 1932,
Linwood frontage was purchased and a large auditorium
was added.

The pulpit and altar rail were fashioned of walnut said to
be intended for World War I gunstocks.

Annunciation Roman Catholic Church

2814 East Linwood Boulevard
1903-1924

Architect:
Frederick C. Gunn

Father William Dalton founded Annunciation Parish and built a church in the West Bottoms in 1872. The flood of 1881 was catastrophic to the congregation, many of whom lost their homes. Father Dalton was given the task of organizing and building a new church at Linwood and Benton boulevards.

The first mass was said to be held in a tent in June 1902, and a frame church was built in 1903 around a cornerstone. Father Dalton believed in "pay as you go" and only built as funds came in. The structure was finally completed in 1924. The original plan for the church called for piers/steeples on the towers. The stained glass windows were made in Innsbruck, Austria.

In 1975 the parishes of Annunciation, Holy Name and St. Vincent were consolidated and renamed Church of the Risen Christ.

St. Peter's Evangelical Church of Christ

3115 East Linwood Boulevard
1924

Architect:
George B. Franklin &
Frank Lloyd Lang

Builder:
L. Breitag & Sons

The original parishioners of St. Peter's Evangelical were comprised of the congregants from the oldest German church in the city, having occupied a site at 13th and Oak for four decades. The organ for the church was given in honor of William Volker and was said to cost $125,000. A new chancel was designed in 1940 and was of the Lutheran style in which space is made on both sides of the altar for a vested choir of forty.

Some of the most prominent details of this church are the large, stained glass windows with tracery in a cut-stone pointed-arch surround, and the gargoyles peering down from the belfry. The Jamison Memorial Temple re-dedicated the church in 1968 and now serves the African-American community.

Central Christian Church

3801 East Linwood Boulevard
1945-1946

Architect:
Robin A. Walker

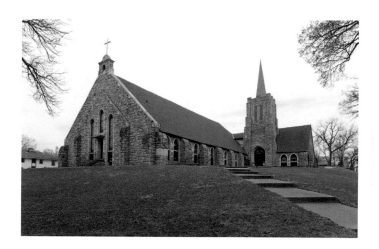

Situated at the corner of Linwood and Cleveland atop
a slight hill, Central Christian Church is a side-steeple
limestone structure with late Gothic Revival elements.
The church's western façade features 18 cut-stone
pointed-arch fenestrations with stained glass in the upper portions of each window, allowing for rich afternoon
light to flood the sanctuary.

Central Christian Church was established in 1889 and
moved into its home on Linwood in 1945.

Wabash Avenue Church of God
(St. Paul's Reformed Presbyterian)

3551 Wabash Avenue
1908-1909

Architect: Builder:
Frank A. Sherrill   C.K. Musselman

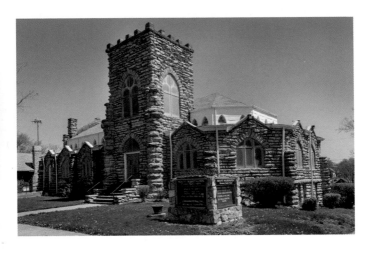

The main façade of this church is dominated by a
two-and-one-half-story crenelated tower through which
congregants enter the sanctuary. The main entrance
consists of wood paneled double doors below an arched
transom set into another arch constructed with prominent stone voussoirs and a keystone. Additional primary
façade fenestration is tripartite arched windows set into
distinct arched surrounds and divided by buttressing.
Each bay is further accentuated by a gabled parapet.

Blessed Sacrament Church

3901 Agnes Avenue
1927

Architect:
Archer & Gloyd

Builder:
George Ginter

Two of the most prominent features of this Romanesque Revival church are its enormous rose window on the main façade and the 132-foot-tall square bell tower on the north façade. Other distinctive elements include Ionic columns between the paired clerestory windows as well as in the bell tower fenestrations, and a terra cotta roof.

Architects Arthur Archer and Galen Gloyd designed the Blessed Sacrament Church in the traditional basilica style. The interior walls and ceilings of the church were hand-stenciled by Dante Cosentino, Sr., an artist who used his earnings to purchase a small fruit stand with the intention of having his children run the business. Cosentino's fruit stand eventually grew into a chain of grocery stores throughout the city, and memories of Dante's angel-covered ceiling at Blessed Sacrament still linger in the minds of former parishioners.

Prospect Avenue Presbyterian Church - Congregation Tefereth Israel

4238 Prospect Avenue
1917

Architect:
James Oliver Hogg (1917)
Bloomgarten & Frohwerk (1935)

This Art Deco church was constructed in 1917 and designed by James Oliver Hogg. Its current appearance came after a remodel in 1935, after it was sold to the Congregation Tefereth Sforad in 1929. Stylized geometric forms flank the doors and parapet over the entranceway. A band of concrete follows the coping of the wall. Stone string courses and bandings of dark brown brick are located along the front and side facades. This church is a good example of the early work of Bloomgarten and Frohwerk, who were known for their modern designs after World War II.

Victor Beutner Residence

1311 Manheim Street
1911

Builder:
Victor Beutner

An example of the Prairie School style, this house is built of poured concrete clad in stucco. Beutner was the head of a concrete company, and designed the home to exemplify a fire-proof residence – once advertised as "The Danger-Proof House." Its east wing strongly resembles Frank Lloyd Wright's Design for the Unity Temple in Oak Park, Illinois.

Immanuel Lutheran Church

4201 Tracy Avenue
1924

Architect:
Philip T. Drotts

Construction on Immanuel Lutheran Church began in 1924, when the basement was built and dedicated, but construction of the superstructure did not begin until 1931. While the building itself is an attractive example of late Gothic Revival design, the church's alter screen and stained-glass windows are stunning works of art.

Ten tripartite windows line the nave of the church, each set into pointed arch fenestrations. The largest set of windows faces north and features a portrait of Martin Luther imported from Germany. Above the choir loft is the Ascension window, a round window donated by the Dorcas Society. Money was raised for the window with a "Sunshine Fund," in which Society members deposited a penny in a contribution box for every day that the sun shined.

D. W. Newcomer & Sons Funeral Home

1331 Brush Creek Boulevard
1925 (add. 1936)

Architect:
Edward Buehler Delk

Landscape Architects:
Hare & Hare

Builders:
Gray-Parker Building, Co.
Collins Bothers

Italian and Spanish influences are apparent in this funeral home, which was viewed as a departure from the usual massive, somber style in mortuary architecture. The building is low and rambling with a roof of Spanish clay and walls of hand troweled gray stucco. Fountains enhance the north end and south entrance, and the grounds are landscaped into a formal Italian garden.

The Newcomer Company was founded in 1893 by David W. Newcomer. The company is said to have been the first to use motorized vehicles for funerals, having introduced that service in 1915.

Paseo Methodist Church (St. James United Methodist)

5539 Paseo
1948

Architect:
Richard N. Wakefield

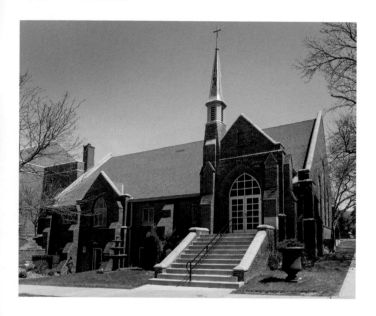

Paseo Methodist Church began its life as a small, stucco chapel in 1924 and was enlarged in 1926. After merging with St. Paul Methodist Episcopal later that same year, the congregation eventually purchased the lot at 56th and Paseo. The present church was not built until 1948, and a large addition was constructed in 1959.

The addition, designed by architect Richard N. Wakefield, was built in strict regard to the original materials and features, and carries the integrity of the church's original design.

Maud Gray Homes

5612 Paseo
1924

Builder:
Maud Gray and D.G. Parker, Gray-Parker Building Co.

Maud Gray was a female contractor/builder who lived and worked in Kansas City at the beginning of the 20th century. Gray was responsible for the construction of nearly 50 homes in the city, first on her own, building approximately ten homes between 3016 and 3036 Walrond (in the Santa Fe Place Historic District) in 1914, six homes on the 3300 block of College in 1916, and twelve homes on the 5700 block of Forest between 1917 and 1918.

Gray went on to join D.G. Parker in the Gray-Parker building Company, and in 1924-1925 they built fourteen more homes along the 5600 block of Paseo. Parker was finally partnered with her sister (as bookkeeper), Mabel, for a handful of homes on the 5600 block of Lydia.

This clapboard residence (pictured above) with stone trim is typical of the bungalow style popular in the 1920s.

St. George's Parish House (John McDowell Trimble Residence)

1600 East 58th Street
1904

Architect:
Arthur Kriehn

Builder:
C.A. Kelly

John McDowell Trimble was born in Rockbridge, Virginia, in 1851. He attended Westminster College in Fulton, Missouri and practiced in Mexico, Missouri, before coming to Kansas City in 1887. He was president of the Kansas City Bar association in 1886 and a member of the University Club. He ran for Missouri governor in 1896 as a Missouri Gold Democrat. The Trimble house is a good example of the Tudor Revival style. This house is clad in limestone with detailed half timbering in the gable ends. There is an arched stone portico on the south façade.

This house was deeded to the St. George Episcopal Church. The building served as its meeting place until the congregation constructed the main sanctuary to the east of the house in 1955. The gothic revival stone church uses the same limestone and has an arched entry to reflect the design of the house.

Philip Rollheiser Residence

1707 59th Street
1936

Builder:
Frank Kraft

One of a pair of cut stone, brick, and stucco residences is this especially charming example of the English Cottage style built here in the 1930s. The style is seen extensively in the south and southeast areas of the city, which were largely developed during this period.

Boone-Hays Cemetery

63rd Street & Euclid Avenue

Daniel Morgan Boone is one of the six sons of Daniel Boone. The Boones moved from Kentucky to Missouri in 1799. In 1825, Boone took a job as an agriculturist for the government, teaching Kaw Indians how to farm. In 1831, he bought a large tract of land and built a log house near present day 63rd Street and Holmes. On June 13, 1839, Daniel Morgan Boone died of cholera at his farm.

The City of Kansas City Parks and Recreation Department acquired the land where Boone was buried in 2002, and the Boone-Hays Cemetery was first dedicated by Native Sons and Daughters of Greater Kansas City in June 2005.

Benedictine Sanctuary of Perpetual Adoration

1409 Meyer Boulevard
1947-1949

Architects:
Joseph B. Shaughnessy, Sr.; Edwin L. Bowers

Builder:
J.E. Dunn

On a lofty hill above the rumble of traffic stands a three-story Neo-Romanesque style building of buff and red brick, which houses a community of Catholic nuns. The convent includes both living quarters and a chapel, beside which stands its campanile. The nuns are members of the order of Benedictine Sisters of Perpetual Adoration, founded in the United States in 1875.

6901 Troost Avenue
1888; 1921-1922 (Pantheon)

Architect:
Sidney Lovell, Chicago

Builder:
Pratt-Thompson Construction

Forest Hill is a notable resting place of many prominent Kansas Citians, including William K. Mulkey, one of Kansas City's earliest settlers and the first developer of the Westside area. Landscaped by George E. Kessler and planted by George Law and Sid Hare, the cemetery's rolling acreage contains more than 90 varieties of American, European and Asian trees.

This massive building inspired by the tombs of ancient Egypt was constructed of reinforced concrete and coated with gray Georgia marble. Contributing to the grandeur of this structure are the handsome bronze entrance doors.

Paseo Christian Church

7201 Paseo
1926; add. 1935

Architect:
Boller Brothers

This Gothic Revival stone church was designed by
Boller Brothers architecture firm. This firm was widely
known for its theater designs, but this is one of the few
churches attributed to them. Paseo Christian is located
in the Marlborough area and was built to reflect the
growing residential growth in the area during the early
20th century.

The church is L-shaped with a sanctuary facing the
Paseo (built in 1926) and a classroom wing facing East
72nd Street (built in 1935.) The building's main entrance
is on the south façade with a small gable portico that
has leaded glass windows and decorative half timbering in the gable end. There is a three-story tower with a
flat roof that connects the two corners of the buildings.
The church was purchased by the Grace Baptist Church
1991.

St. John Seminary

2001 72nd Street
1930

Architect:
Maurice Carroll;
O'Meara & Hills

Builder:
Matthew Rauen, Chicago

Considered to be the biggest undertaking in the history of the Kansas City Diocese, St. John Seminary began as an idea in 1883 but was not built until 1930. Bishop Thomas Lillis spoke at every single parish in the diocese to raise money for the seminary; every parish tithed and every priest contributed until $600,000 had been raised.

The architectural firm O'Meara and Hills of St. Louis, who had established a reputation as specialists in Roman Catholic ecclesiastical work, was contracted to design the structure, and Gottfried Schiller, also of St. Louis, decorated the interior. In 1935, to celebrate the Golden Jubilee of the career of Bishop Lillis, windows designed by St. Louis stained glass artist Emil Frie were installed. The windows depict the life and history of a priest.

St. John Seminary closed in 1983 and now houses a charter school.

Marlborough Area

75th Street to 79th Street
Troost Avenue to Prospect Avenue

The T. B. Potter Realty Company platted the first development in this area in 1907. Developer William B. Clarke named the new streetcar suburb "Marlborough Heights" in honor of John Churchill, the first Duke of Marlborough. Promotional material described the area as "Kansas City's New Residence Park," boasting 100-foot wide lots, electric lights, city water services, and an electric streetcar line that connected the garden suburb to the city center. The residents of Marlborough Heights and the other subdivisions that followed shortly thereafter supported the businesses that operated in Marlborough Village.

The northern portions of Marlborough were annexed in 1909 and the Marlborough Village commercial center in 1947. This area has a wide range of architectural styles. The first houses were those large country houses on large lots promoted by Clark, later in the early 20th century smaller revival style homes were built, and finally a post-World War II building boom filled in the remaining lots with ranch houses.

The Paseo Viaducts

77th Street and Paseo
1925-1926

Architect:
Harrington, Howard & Ash,
Engineers

Developers:
D. Munro; H.H. Hannebratt

These twin viaducts of Neoclassical design originally served both vehicular and streetcar traffic. Constructed of reinforced concrete, the gracefully arched bridges span 77th Street.

Ellis Hall (Dodson District)

2510 East 85th Street

c. 1927

This Neoclassical brick commercial building played an important role in the life of Dodson, Missouri, a small industrial community centered around 85th and Prospect Streets and annexed by Kansas City in 1947. Originally, the building was the home of Alonzo E. Ellis and served also as the Dodson post office during Ellis' tenure as postmaster. Dodson was the southernmost point on the Westport Belt Line, a rail line generally referred to as "The Dummy," which extended from Westport through Waldo to Dodson.

Hare Residences

7119 & 7120 Harecliff Drive
1925 & 1921

Architect: Developer:
Sid J. Hare   Sid J. Hare

Hare, a nationally known landscape architect, built the house at 7120 for himself and the residence across the street for his daughter, Nell Hare Stevenson.

The architect's highly personal home, which he called Timber Tent, was built on 20 rugged acres known as Harecliff. Bridge timbers 8 inches thick form the walls of the house. The foundation is composed of stoned quarried on the property, and the chimney is built of water-worn surface rock from a cliff top that extends the width of the property.

Years earlier, the surrounding area had served as a campground for Santa Fe Trail pioneers, who refreshed themselves at Cave Springs, a small limestone cave where a tiny spring trickles out at Gregory Boulevard and Blue River extension.

Swope Park Memorial and Mausoleum

6900 Swope Memorial Drive
1916-1917

Architect:
Wight & Wight

In 1918 the body of Thomas H. Swope was placed in a crypt beneath this Neoclassical style marble portico flanked by recumbent lions. Inscribed on the bronze plaque is the following: "His wisdom conceived, his generosity gave to the people of Kansas City this noble expanse of field and forest for their perpetual enjoyment."

Van Noy Residences

6700 & 6800 Elmwood Avenue
1909

Architect:
Clifton B. Sloan

The Elmwood Avenue homes were built in 1909 for Ira C. Van Noy and Charles Van Noy respectively. The Van Noy brothers ran a successful news distribution and cigar retail business that supplied the railways. Their business would eventually control the distribution of media and cigars for the Missouri Pacific, Western Pacific, Iron Mountain and Southern, Kansas City Southern and Illinois Central railways. When these homes were originally built they were outside the city limits.

The 6700 house reflects the country-estate feel with its English Tudor architecture and American eclectic ele-

ments. The three-story home includes a carriage house and small lake on the property. The 6800 house is a two-story Italianate-style home with a stone exterior.

Swope Park Shelter House #1

6601 Swope Parkway
1904

Architect:
Adriance Van Brunt

The park superintendent's quarters were on the second floor of this rather elegant Spanish Mission style shelter house, constructed of squared fieldstone and flanked by twin three-story observation towers and pergolas.

Swope Park Swimming Pool

6700 Lewis Road
1941

Architect:
Marshall & Brown

The Swope Park Pool complex was constructed as a Works Progress Administration (WPA) project sponsored by the city through the Board of Park Commissioners. The complex, including the handsome wrought iron entrance gates, was seen as "a modern, beautiful country club for the family . . . created . . . at a negligible cost to the taxpayer."

Byram's Ford

63rd Street & Blue River
1864

Byram's Ford was a 19th century crossing of the Big Blue River on the Independence to Westport Road. During the Confederate invasion of Missouri by the forces of Maj. Gen. Sterling Price in 1864, Byram's Ford was the scene of two separate battles.

Price was in Independence with his Confederate Army and a train of more than 500 wagons. Ahead of him, deployed along the Big Blue River, was a large Union force, while behind him in pursuit was another large Union cavalry force. On Saturday, October 22, Price defeated the Union forces guarding Byram's Ford and was able to cross the Big Blue River there, sending his wagon train on to New Santa Fe. On Sunday, October 23, Price deployed some of his Confederate forces at Byram's Ford to prevent the Union cavalry pursuit from overtaking the Confederate wagon train. The Union forces attacked and defeated the Confederate defenders at Byram's Ford, who retreated south to protect the wagon train. This, combined with the Confederate defeat south of Brush Creek, marked an end to the three-day Battle of Westport.

Swope Park Christian Church

6140 Swope Parkway
1913-1914

Architect:
Samuel B. Tarbet

Builder:
Wallace T. Thornberg

Swope Park Christian Church is a Late Gothic Revival, twin-towered structure built from local stone. What sets this church apart from other churches in the region that were designed in the same style is not the outside, but the inside.

On August 14, 1979, a fire destroyed The West Paseo Christian Church nearly 6 miles northwest of Swope Park Christian Church. West Paseo Christian was a predominantly black congregation that was formed around 1875. Following the fire, Swope Park Christian, with a mostly white congregation, invited West Paseo Christian to worship in their church, eventually leading to a joint worship service. Just three months later, the two churches voted to become one congregation – Swope Park United Christian Church.

Swope Park Lodge
AF & AM No. 617

5934 Swope Parkway
1922; alt. 1944

Architect:
George W. Swehla

Builders:
Gillham, Cook & White,
Mechanical Engineers, K.C.
Structural Steel

The structure at 5934 Swope Parkway began its life as a Freemason's temple. The Classical Revival temple features two wide corner bays with pilasters that support a prominent pediment with a single oculus. A continuous watertable rests below the pediment.

During the Great Depression and war, the lodge fell on hard times. The building was sold to the St. Louis Catholic Church on June 1, 1944. When the congregation purchased the church, the interior was finished, and the church was dedicated in September 1945.

Church of the Covenant

5931 Swope Parkway
1914; alt. 1928-1929

Architect:
Saylor, Owen & Payson (1928-1929)

The unusual plan of this church, designed in installments, was to complete half of the building at a time. The chapel in the polygon-shaped unit was the first to be completed in 1915. The entire building was completed and dedicated in January 1929.

An addition was constructed in 1952 and designed by architect Sigmund H. Sieben.

Wheatley Public School

5332 South Benton Avenue

Wheatley Public School, a two-room school building, served the surrounding African-American community. The site originally consisted of two one-room structures and this two-room structure. The other buildings were demolished after the students were integrated into the Graceland School on 51st Street. This craftsman style building was a typical temporary building that provided class space while a new building was under construction. These simple buildings were built by the school district and rarely had electricity or plumbing. The Wheatley building could have easily been on multiple sites before ending up in this location. A church purchased the school after it was closed and constructed the central tower.

Robert H. Fitzgerald Residence

4761 Eastwood Drive
c. 1918

Builder:
Swofford Realty Co.

The forested terrain of Eastwood Hills made this one
of Kansas City's most delightful suburbs. Typical of the
commodious yet modest residences is this one-and-one-
half-story frame house built on extensive landscaped
grounds.

In 1915, the Swofford Mortgage and Investment Company started developing the Eastwood Hills subdivision.
The neighborhood was marketed as a "charming restricted residential community." The neighborhood had
views to the downtown and surrounding areas because
of it being situated on the highest elevation at the time in
the city.

Fire Station No. 26

6402 Stadium Drive
1911

Architect:
Owen & Payson

The crisp herringbone brickwork above the doorways
and atop the pylons is typical of the tapestry brick design
that grew in popularity across America. This station
served the industrial Leeds district. Fire alarms were
often turned in by "certain young women who desired to
see their favorite Irish heroes thunder by on the fire-
wagons."

Santa Fe Trail

East 27th Street & Topping Avenue

Thinly covered with grass, the Santa Fe Trail etched by pioneers more than 100 years ago is still discernible. This section of the trail is a narrow and shallow depression that runs diagonally into the woods at the intersection of Topping Avenue and 27th Street.

This branch of the trail left Independence, Missouri, went through Westport and on to Santa Fe. It was used not for passenger service but for freighting goods.

Church of God, Holiness

2844 Askew Avenue
1917

Architect:
Ernest O. Brostrom

Architect E.O. Brostrom designed this Art Deco church, which was constructed in two stages. The basement was built in 1917 and the superstructure was built in 1928. Bostrom developed a new way of using concrete (stucco over a Con-Tee construction) and used it for the exterior of the building.

The cornerstone of the church reads, "Starlight Missionary Baptist Church organized 1930."

Santa Fe Neighborhood

27th Street to Linwood Boulevard
Prospect Avenue to Indiana Avenue
1897

John Thornton became the first person to file a claim on the 520 acres of land in 1827 known today as the Santa Fe Neighborhood. The land was used as a distillery and grain mill to serve the people on the Santa Fe Trail and those in the Westport and Kansas City areas. In 1835 the land was purchased by Jones and Rachel Lockridge, who had five children and several slaves. Sixty years later, Lockridge relatives began developing an exclusive residential neighborhood called Santa Fe Place. By 1915, Santa Fe had the reputation as "the place to live" for the rich and powerful in Kansas City.

In 1931, the neighborhood created a covenant that "no real estate in Santa Fe Place could be sold, given, rented to or occupied by black people for a period of thirty years." Despite the covenant, in 1948, Dr. D.M. Miller and his wife became the first black family to establish residency in Santa Fe. The Missouri Supreme Court ruled the covenant unconstitutional and illegal in 1949. By the 1950s, affluent African-American families began moving into the neighborhood.

First Swedish Evangelical Faith Church (Pleasant Green Baptist Church)

2910 East 30th Street
1924

Architect:
H.C. Eckland

Builder:
Godfrey Swenson

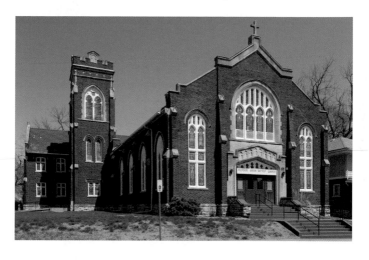

Originally known as the First Swedish Evangelical Faith Church, this building represents a work of unique, picturesque and ornamental craftsmanship. Harmonious massing and a simple silhouette provide a pleasant focal point for the surrounding community.

Polychromy is restricted to a red brick veneer banded by smooth stone trim. Details of molding and carved ornament around doorways, windows and parapets are heavy and sculpted. External woodwork – seen in the tracery windows – is solid and structured. Long, low lines are counterbalanced by vertical accents. Gothic vocabulary is used, but the whole of the church exhibits a greater self-restraint than the High Victorian Gothic style.

Elias L. Pound Residence

2937 Lockridge Avenue
1909

Builder:
Henthorn & Ferguson

Typical of the many comfortable houses built just after the turn of the century, this type of house heralded the start of housing development construction. One of a row of similar houses built for comfort, this two-and-one-half-story fieldstone and shingle "shirtwaist" type residence with a bell cast roof was owned by Elias L. Pound, a cashier for the Studebaker Corporation in Kansas City.

Benton Boulevard Baptist Church
(Macedonia Baptist Church)

2455 Benton Boulevard
1904-1905

Architect:
Edwards & Sunderland

The Benton Boulevard Baptist Church exhibits an early use of concrete block construction. The concrete blocks have been highly polished. This is particularly unique to ecclesiastical buildings of this era. Designed by the architectural firm of Edwards and Sunderland, this church is a good example of the late Gothic Revival style of architecture.

A gymnasium was added in 1921, and in 1955 the Benton Boulevard Baptist Church sold the building to the Macedonia Baptist Church for approximately $45,000.

Park Avenue Evangelical Church (Bowers Memorial Christian Methodist Church)

2456 Park Avenue
1906-1907

Architect:
Rudolf Markgraf

Native limestone used as a building material was popular at the turn of the century. Park Avenue Evangelical Church is representative of the fine local work done in this medium. (Another excellent example is St. Paul's Reformed Presbyterian Church, 3551 Wabash Street.) Unique to this church are the mission-like parapets and undulating lines.

At the time of dedication in 1907, services at the church were conducted in German in the morning and English in the afternoon.

South Prospect Christian Church

2126 Prospect Avenue
1894

Architect:
Frederick E. Hill

The Wabash Christian Church purchased the lot for the present church, which was built in 1894. At the time, the church's name was changed to the South Prospect Christian Church. In 1910 the building was sold to the Arlington Methodist Episcopal Church, and in 1929 it was purchased by the Ward Chapel A.M.E. Church.

Hill designed the church with a Romanesque influence. The south wall has an apse with a semi-conical roof; the western end of the south elevation has two entrances – one with stone voussoirs in a rounded arch frame. There is a stone chimney at the north elevation.

Elmwood Cemetery

4900 Truman Road
est. 1875; 1925 (office)

Architect:
Wight & Wight (office building)

Landscape Architect:
George Kessler

Builder:
Swenson Construction (office building)

Magnificent wrought-iron gates mark the entrance to
this cemetery. Just inside the gate is a Gothic chapel,
erected in memory of Kirkland B. Armour of the packing house family. The property is comprised of approximately 43 acres of land. The cemetery was named after
the numerous elm trees that exist on the property, and to
this day there is a variety of tree species on the property
that date back to the early days of the cemetery.

The cemetery was commercially owned until 1896, when
lot owners purchased the 40 acres and formed the Elmwood Cemetery Society. The cemetery, resplendent with
funerary art and handsome internment vaults, includes
an exclusively Jewish section where some of the city's
earliest and most prominent Jewish residents are buried.

St. Paul School of Theology

5123 Truman Road
established 1904

This campus was opened in 1904 as the Kansas City National Training School for Deaconesses and Missionaries. In 1933, the name was changed to the National Training School for Christians, and changed again to the National College for Christian Workers in 1945, and then to National College in 1958. The institution explored a cooperative merger with Saint Paul before closing in 1964.

Anna E. Kresge Chapel
1949

Architect:
Hardy & Schumacher

Builder:
H.H. Fox Construction Co.

The chapel was a gift to the school on the condition that the donor's name not be revealed, a condition which was later rescinded. Anna E. Kresge, a Detroit-based philanthropist, left $175,000 to the school.

Kansas Building
1922

Architect:
Shepard & Wiser

East Kensington Cottages

1622-1638 Poplar Avenue

The East Kensington subdivision was platted in 1887 by Christian E. Schoellkopf, a German immigrant. While platted 20 years earlier, the 1600 block of Poplar wasn't developed until 1907. Like many subdivisions, various builders and developers purchased lots to build homes. Frank T. Buckingham, Carl Vrooman, Berrien H. Finlay, and Allen & Robinson were the main builders on this block. These homes were built for the working and middle class of Kansas City. A review of the city directories shows that the early occupants worked as stenographers for the Faultless Engine Co., a telephone operator for Morris & Company and a contractor.

These vernacular cottages feature unique bell-cast eaves, hipped roofs, shed dormers, and decorative brackets. The first stories are brick with arches lintels atop the window openings. The houses have a unique character that is not common in Kansas City and demonstrates the creativity of builders, even on these modest homes.

Centropolis Baptist Church 65

1410 White Avenue
1927; add. 1948

Architects:
Ferrand & Fitch (1927)
B.A. Larson (1948)

Builder:
D & L Engineering &
Construction Co. (1948)

Excavation was begun in 1926 for the erection of a two-story and basement structure, and the building was completed in 1927. Originally intended to be used exclusively as a Sunday school, the basement housed the kitchen, dining room and school rooms, while the main floor housed a temporary auditorium, and the second floor housed 42 additional school rooms.

The church auditorium was built in 1948 and features Gothic elements including multi-light art glass set into pointed arches along the east and west facades. Until recently, a large, multi-light, art glass rounded arch window was visible above the centrally placed entrance, but is now boarded over.

St. Stephen Catholic Church

1028 Bennington Avenue
1909

Architect:
William E. Brown

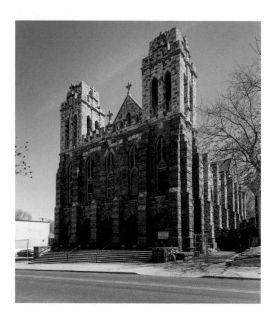

The original St. Stephan Church and school (1888, 1889) facility burned in 1913. The stone foundation from the original church was refitted to form temporary quarters for the congregation. Plans for the church progressed despite the war slowing the progress. The church was finally dedicated on September 6, 1925.

Due to high unemployment and an empty treasury, much of the church was rebuilt by members of the congregation. Materials were donated, and parishioner Michael E. Reiser frescoed some of the interior murals.

In 1992 the Diocese closed St. Stephen and three other churches and created Our Lady of Peace Parish, which is located on the St. Stephen campus.

Holy Trinity Catholic Church

930 Norton Avenue
1926

Architect:
H.W. Brinkman

Builder:
N.F. Gosche

Founded in 1889, Holy Trinity is the second church of the parish, as the first, built at 7th and Cypress, burned down twice. Two white alcoves accent the street-facing façade's red brick exterior. The alcoves once contained Carrera marble statues, one of the Sacred Heart, and one of the Blessed Mother. The church's twin Italianate-influenced towers each feature white bracket cornices with supporting white pilasters. These pilasters, in turn, support a series of brick arches that decorate each tower's faux belvedere belfry. The nave features four large, arched windows, which formerly contained art glass windows depicting the mysteries of the Rosary. In 1991, the dioceses consolidated the parish with the St. Michael, St. Steven, and St. Stanislaus parishes. Holy Trinity's congregation celebrated its final Mass on February 3, 1991.

Bales Baptist Church

3412 12th Street
1915

Architect:
Shepard, Farrar & Wiser

The site for this church was donated by the Bales family in 1895 and the cornerstone was laid April 13, 1916. The roof was designed as a decked roof arranged as a roof garden so that summer services could be held outside.

Dorson Apartments

912-918 Benton Boulevard
1906

Builder:
R.L. Dawson Construction Co.

Corinthian columns and wrought-iron balustrades grace
the facade of this elegantly interpreted apartment house.
The three-story building reflects a colonnade style that
was prolific enough to be deemed the "Kansas City
Colonnade."

Olive Street Baptist Church

905 Olive Street
c. 1885

Built in 1885, this Gothic style church is quite eclectic in design. Perhaps the most interesting element of the church is the polygonal tower unit with brick buttressing and amortizements at the northwest corner of the building. A paired, pointed, multipaned arch unit is placed in a pointed arch lintel with keystones and screwbacks. Parapet ends on the west/main façade feature fixed, pointed arch windows placed within pointed-arch brick surrounds with keystones and lug sills.

Central Baptist
Church of God in Christ

2310 East 10th Street
1911

Architect:
Francis E. Parker & Sons

As a result of the reorganization of two churches (Olive Street and Emmanuel) the Central Baptist Church was formed in 1907 during the pastorate of Reverend J.S. Davis. The first $2,000 toward the construction of a new church was raised in 1907-1909. In June 1911, construction of the new church began under the pastorate of Reverend Roluix Harlan. Reverend and Dr. W.S. Abernathy dedicated this church on November 17, 1912. The cost of the building was reported to be $28,000.

Metropolitan Spiritual Church of Christ

1231 Garfield Avenue
1886

The original portion of this church, which faces Garfield Avenue, was a private residence from its construction (circa 1886) until 1926, when the building was purchased by the Metropolitan Spiritual Church. That year a rear addition was constructed, significantly enlarging the Italianite style residence at its east elevation.

In 1933, another addition was made to the east, and the front portico and garage were constructed in 1946. The portico features a wide entablature supported by five large Doric styled columns.

Beacon Light Seventh Day Adventist Church

1226 Euclid Avenue
1942-1943

Architect:
John Frederick Granstedt

Builder:
R.L. Evans; Rev. A.E. Webb

The Beacon Light Seventh Day Adventist Church was dedicated on November 27, 1943. Local architect John F. Granstedt designed the church, and Reverend A.E. Webb, minister of the church, assisted in the construction, which spanned two years. The limestone and steel of the church were salvaged from the old Muehlebach brewery and other wrecking sites.

Dr. G.L. Henderson Residence

1016 Paseo
1899

Architect:
Rudolf Markgraf

At the turn of the century, The Paseo was one of the city's most elegant boulevards. It was so fashionable that Kansas City residents such as Dr. Generous L. Henderson were attracted away from other choice neighborhoods, in his case Mulkey Square, to build new houses here. In 1899, the same year in which the elegant brick and stone Henderson residence was constructed, the Pergola between 10th and 11th Streets was added to The Paseo Boulevard system.

St. Stephen Baptist Church

1414 Truman Road
1913; 1945

Architect:
Owen & Payson (1913)
Ernest O. Brostrom (1945)

Builder:
Doty & Son (1913)
W.C. White, San Antonio, TX (1945)

This buff brick church, modernistic in style, has been a place of worship for one of the nation's largest black Baptist congregations. The church was established in 1903 when Rev. J.W. Hurse, its founder, held services from his wagon. In 1921, members moved to a structure at 910 Harrison. The church on Harrison Street

was destroyed by fire in 1938. Rev. R.J. Jordan, then pastor, purchased the Paseo Dance Hall located at Truman Road and The Paseo in 1941. The hall was reconditioned and served as the church until the present $250,000 structure was constructed on the same site in 1945. St. Stephen's congregation remains a very active force in the black community.

St. Monica Mission Church

1400 East 17th Street
1913

Architect:
Horace LaPierre

Builder:
K.C. Construction Co.

With a donation of $8,000 and smaller gifts, Father Cyprian purchased a lot at the northeast corner of 17th and Lydia Streets, which included four houses. Three of the homes were rented, and the income from these properties was used to supplements the donations to build the church. The remaining house was remodeled and used as a church and a school.

The first service was held on October 16, 1910. Three years later, in 1913, a two-story school and chapel were constructed. All that remains of the original house and school is this property, which is now owned by St. Joseph Church.

Crossroads
Midtown
Westport

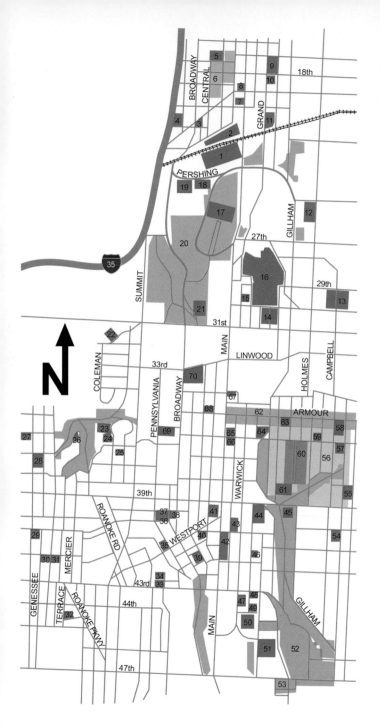

1. Union Station
2. Chicago, Milwaukee & St. Paul RR Freight House
3. Broadway Bank
4. Jensen-Salsbury Laboratory, Inc
5. Webster School
6. Film Row
7. Michael's Clothing Building
8. Pendergast Headquarters
9. Kansas City Star Building
10. City Bank Building
11. Western Auto
12. Commercial Buildings
13. Longfellow Residences
14. Union Hill Residences
15. J.W. Axtell Residence
16. Union Cemetery
17. Liberty Memorial
18. Sweeney Auto School
19. U.S. Post Office
20. Penn Valley Park
21. Penn Valley Park Maintenance Building
22. J.B. Fugate Residence
23. Clarence W. Sondern Residence
24. Thomas Hart Benton Residence
25. Joseph H. Rush Residence
26. Norman Tromanhauser Residence
27. Willard G. Kenerson Residence
28. William Volker Residence
29. Roanoke United Methodist Church
30. Roanoke Presbyterian Church
31. Swedish Evangelical Mission Church
32. Emil J. Rohrer Residence
33. Heider-James Residence
34. St. James Baptist Church
35. Albert G. Boone's Store
36. Westport United Methodist Church
37. Our Lady of Good Counsel Church
38. Broadway Baptist Church
39. Rev. Nathan Scarritt Residence
40. John Harris Residence
41. First Calvary Baptist Church
42. St. Paul's Episcopal Church
43. Third Church of Christ, Scientist
44. Westport High School
45. Gillham Park Maintenance Building
46. William C. Schmidt Residence
47. George C. Wright Residence
48. The Zurn Colonnades
49. R.E. Bruner Residence - Mineral Hall
50. August R. Meyer Residence
51. Nelson-Atkins Museum of Art
52. Rockhill Neighborhood
53. Pierce Street Homes
54. United Bretheren Church
55. St. Mark Lutheran Church
56. Hyde Park Neighborhood
57. James H. Harkless Residence
58. Central Presbyterian Church
59. Charles E. Granniss Residence
60. Janssen Place
61. Notre Dame de Sion School
62. Apartment Buildings on Armour
63. Newbern Apartments
64. William M. Reid Residence
65. William Knight Residence
66. Westminster Congregational Church
67. Longmeadow Historic District
68. West Armour Apartments
69. Knickerbocker Apartments
70. Redemptorist Church

Crossroads
Midtown
Westport

It was not long before industrial success and population growth forced late 19th century Kansas City to expand its borders. Residential neighborhoods cropped up near the rocky bluffs east and southwest of the urban and commercial centers, leaving the area directly south of downtown ripe for new commercial construction. This growth was not haphazard. Officials engaged experts to plan and develop parks and boulevards befitting a city that aspired for civic beauty to match its industrial prominence. Slowly expanding southward, the Crossroads and especially Midtown districts drew the city closer to Westport, an independent municipality originally established as a pioneer trading post in the 1830s. In 1897, the rechristened Kansas City annexed Westport, adding a historically and architecturally distinct district to the burgeoning metropolis.

The old town of West Port served the needs of Santa Fee trail migrants seeking a new life in the West. Isaac McCoy, a Baptist missionary, settled the area in 1831. The 1840s and '50s were a boom time for Westport. Pioneers on the Santa Fe Trail, many seeking Oregon land or California gold, passed through and purchased supplies brought to McCoy's shop from the river landing a few miles north. Compared to Independence, Missouri, the other main point of westward departure, wagon trains leaving from Westport did not have to ford the Blue River and could take advantage of plentiful grazing for their oxen. Pioneers and traders recognized these advantages and flocked to Westport. By 1855, the settlement reached a peak population of 5,000 and officially incorporated in 1857.

From its apex in the mid-1850s, two related factors reduced Westport's local power and influence: the coming Civil War and Kansas City's resulting regional ascendency. Civil War came early on the border, as the partisan skirmishes over Kansas's entry as a Free State or Slave State created an inhospitable environment for would be pioneers. What the Border War reduced, the Civil War destroyed – the Santa Fe Trail trade fell off one quarter by the spring of 1861, and functionally ceased that autumn. Once hostilities started, uneven federal intervention forever altered the balance of power in the region. Union forces occupied southern-sympathizing Westport, while the neighboring City of Kansas received substantial federal investments. When construction began on the Hannibal Bridge – the first railroad bridge to span the Missouri River – near Kansas City in 1867, it became clear that Westport was no longer the regional metropolis.

The expansion of Kansas City into the Westport vicinity did not happen all at once, but instead was the result of a considered and planned civic development. City officials, conscientious that Kansas City be not only an industrial powerhouse but also a great city of parks and culture, pursued a plan to develop the city under the prevailing City Beautiful ideology. In 1892, the City Park Board hired George E. Kessler to design a city plan featuring scenic parks linked by grand boulevards. Kessler, a German émigré and internationally sought after city planner and landscape architect, presented a comprehensive plan to the Parks Board in 1893. Inspired by Kessler's grand designs, the Parks Board granted broad powers to officials to evict working-class squatters from the area that would become Penn Valley Park. Beyond parks boulevards, other developments in line with the City Beautiful plan for the Midtown and Crossroads districts included the first Kansas City Star Building (1911), Union Station (1914), and the Liberty Memorial (1926).

After experiencing the monumental growth that justified the annexation of Westport in 1897, the fortunes of
the Westport-Midtown-Crossroads districts stabilized
through the early 20th century before receiving serious
body blows after World War II. First, air travel reduced
the need for Union Station, eventually rendering that
once grand structure a leaky urban ruin. Second, dein-
dustrialization generated a spate of derelict buildings in
the once prosperous Crossroads manufacturing district.
When the transportation and industrial base crumbled,
much of the surrounding business infrastructure moved
out of the city, following the middle-classes from their
former urban apartments to the suburbs. The decline
damaged much of local business and community. Some
areas, notably Westport, were able to maintain their
status as cultural and entertainment districts.

In spite of all these radical changes, recent efforts to
reclaim and revitalize the neighborhoods have restored
some areas to their former glory. After a historic bi-state
initiative passed in 1996, Union Station underwent a
restoration and transformation, from dilapidated colossus
to celebrated locale featuring restaurants, shops, and a
large exhibition space. Likewise, historic preservation-
ists have leveraged tax initiatives to convert some of the
Crossroads district's many vacant industrial buildings
into loft apartments. Similar gentrification projects have
restored several once prominent Midtown apartment
buildings to their early 20th century grandeur. These encouraging trends demonstrate that Kansas Citians value
preserving and maintaining our shared architectural
heritage.

Union Station

Pershing Road at Main Street
1910-1914

Architect:
Jarvis Hunt, Chicago

Builder:
Fuller Construction Co.

Possibly the most photographed building in Kansas
City, the monumental Union Station is considered the
city's most prominent architectural contribution to the
City Beautiful movement. Prominent Chicago architect
Jarvis Hunt proposed a T-shaped six-story building in the
Beaux Arts Classic style to replace the old Union Depot
in West Bottoms (which was demolished upon comple-
tion of the new station.)

The structure was designed to face southeast. Constructed of gray-white Bedford limestone and polished
New England granite, it is reminiscent of the large-scale
spaces and façade treatments of a Roman bath. Three
major arches, each nearly 90 feet in height, create a vast
openness on the front (south) façade.

The interior space is just as magnificent as the exterior, featuring a 240 x 100 foot ticket lobby with a 108-foot ceiling. The waiting room – now an open space – features numerous doorways in which passengers connect by means of stairways and escalators to the tracks below. Marble in varying warm, rosy-brown shades is used as the predominant finish on floors and walls. The original light fixtures and fittings are still in place. The rooms have heavily coffered, ornamental plaster ceilings.

Kansas City's Union Station Station remains one of the largest railroad stations in the world.

Chicago, Milwaukee & St. Paul Railroad Freight House

101 W. 22nd Street
1888

This long, two-story rectangular load-bearing redbrick structure may currently house restaurants, but its past life as a railroad freight house is apparent at first glance. Though closed off with glass windows, many of the south façade's former access points for loading and unloading freight are easily discernable. Located between warehouses and factories to the north and Union Station to the southeast, the freight house served as an intermediary staging area for railroad shipping. Opened in 1888, the freight house predominately served the Chicago, Milwaukee and St. Paul Railroad, a considerable player in Midwestern rail transit dating from 1847. The building underwent major renovations in 1998. A pedestrian bridge over the railroad tracks now connects the freight house to Union Station.

Broadway Bank

2045 Broadway Boulevard
c. 1888

Even though this building has served a variety of commercial firms over the years, the name Broadway Bank has stayed with the building since the 1920s.

Situated on a corner and occupying frontage on both Broadway and Southwest Boulevard, the building's main facades consist of storefronts on the first story. The second story is fenestrated with a row of rectangular windows, above which is placed a series of roundrels. The parapet wall is castellated. The first floor is veneered with stone. However, the building has undoubtedly undergone alterations.

Jensen-Salsbery Laboratories, Inc. 4

520 W 21st Street
1918; add. 1946

Architect:
Ernest O. Brostrom

Builder:
Morris Hoffman Construction
Co. (1946-47)

The Prairie School design of this three-story masonry commercial structure features a strong horizontal massing with piers and mullions lending vertical accents to the mass. Notable features of the design include carved caryatid figures within the central bay, visually supporting the parapet, and the ornamental brickwork along the third-story level.

Jensen-Salsbery Laboratories, commonly referred to as Jen-Sal, was founded in 1913. It has grown to international prominence as one of the leading producers and suppliers of veterinary pharmaceuticals and biological medicines.

Webster School

1644 Wyandotte Street
1885; add. 1887

Architect:
Manuel A. Diaz (1885)

Builder:
Mumma & Wood (1885)

The Webster School has both historic and stylistic significance. Historically, the school is one of the oldest extant "scientifically" designed Kansas City Public School buildings. The Webster School (and its ten siblings) were the first Kansas City schools designed to "scientifically" aid instruction. Manuel A. Diaz, the school board architect, designed the school buildings considering how heating, lighting, seating, and ventilation would influence student learning. Opening in 1886, the school served a working-class neighborhood for 45 years before closing in 1932.

The school was constructed in a distinctive style known as Richardsonian Romanesque. The style blended French, Spanish, and Italian elements, was most popular between 1880–1900, and was characterized by an eclectic use of proportion, line, and form to create whimsical but weighty designs. A few of the school's design features include contrasting gray stone belts, a double-peaked roof on the front façade, narrow fenestrations, a pyramid belvedere, and round towers.

Film Row

Baltimore Avenue to Central Street
17th Street to 20th Street

Kansas City's connections to the film industry do not stop with Walt Disney, Jean Harlow, and the Mainstreet Theater; it also has a rich history of feature film distribution. Centered on the intersection of 18th and Wyandotte, many major film studios located regional logistics and distribution centers in Kansas City. The list includes powerhouses like Paramount (1800 Wyandotte), Twentieth Century Fox (1716 Wyandotte), Monogram (116 W. 18th St.), United Artists (219 W. 18th St.), and Metro-Goldwyn-Myer (220 W. 18th St.).

Though there was undoubtedly some glamour in working for a major studio, storing and distributing vintage film stock was serious and sometimes dangerous business. Cellulose nitrate, the first popular film base, was highly volatile, and storing large quantities together created

Warner Brothers - Vitagraph Film Exchange

1703 Wyandotte Street
1930

Architect: Zimmerman, Saxe & Zimmerman, Chicago

20th Century Fox
1716 Wyandotte Street
1930

Architect: McKecknie & Trask

serious fire risks. By the 1930s, cellulose nitrate had given way to cellulose acetate, the so-called "safety film." While the new film base was less prone to combustion than the previous nitrate films, storing and transporting large quantities of motion picture stock still required vigilance – especially in a cigarette-friendly era.

United Artists
219 West 18th Street
1931

Architect: Robert F. Gornall

Michael's Clothing

1830 Main Street
c. 1884; alt. 1914, 1948

The earliest known tenant of this building was the Kaw Valley Paint and Oil Company, but it is best known for its longest-lasting tenant – Michael's Fine Clothes for Men, which has occupied the building since 1905. Michael's was originally a pawn shop/men's clothing store owned by a Russian immigrant named Michael H. Novorr. The establishment has remained in the family, ultimately shifting away from the pawn shop to specialize solely in men's clothes, and now four generations of Novorrs have run the business. The store was expanded in 1965 to double the amount of floor space.

Pendergast Headquarters

1908 Main Street

1926

Architect:
R.H. Sanneman

Builder:
Fleming-Gilchrist Construction Co.

This unpretentious two-story buff brick building was the headquarters of one of the most influential men in Kansas City for almost 30 years. It was from here that Thomas Joseph Pendergast ran his political machine. While best known for his political influence, he achieved considerable success in the business world. He headed the Ready Mix Concrete Company and the T. J. Pendergast Wholesale Liquor Company.

Kansas City Star Building

18th Street & Grand Avenue
1909-1911

Architect:
Jarvis Hunt, Chicago

Engineers:
Ritter & Mott, Chicago

William Rockhill Nelson, who founded The Kansas
City Star in 1880, announced the purchase of this site
in 1908 and commissioned Hunt to design a "modern"
printing facility. Hunt selected an Italian Renaissance Revival style with an overhanging cornice and a red clay tile
roof. The steel and concrete frame is faced with tapestry
brick, and a 100-foot water tower unites the two sections
of the building.

City Bank Building

1801-1805 Grand
1926-1927

Architect:	Builder:
Holden, Ferris & Barnes	Eberhardt Construction Co.

Originally planned as a 13-story behemoth, the City
Bank Building instead ended up only seven stories high.
But those seven stories were enough to set the building
apart from its surrounding streetscape. Built in a fringe
district where the Crossroads starts to transition into Midtown, the City Bank Building follows a U-shaped design.
Large towers flank the two-story banking lobby. Unlike
some other U-shaped buildings oriented to present a flat
façade, the City Bank's primary façade exposes the U-
shape. The design further accentuates the U-shape, as
the white stone veneer extends only to the second floor.
Above that floor, the tower's red brick stands in stark
contrast to the contiguous white stone-clad main lobby.
With its Romanesque arches and Neoclassical design,
the City National Bank is something of a holdover from
an older design generation. It has more stylistically in
common with the much older New York Life Building
(1890), than with its chronological peer, the Union Carbide and Carbon Building (1929).

Western Auto

2101-2111 Grand
1914-1915

Architect:
Arthur Tuft, Baltimore

Builder:
Swenson Construction Co.

Built as the local headquarters for the Coca-Cola Company, the building's distinctive shape was the result of an unusual triangle shaped plot of land. Baltimore architect Arthur Tufts used the odd plot to his advantage, designing a triangular building with two straight, right-angled elevations, and a curved southeastern hypotenuse face. Following the dictates of the modern Chicago school, the 12-story reinforced concrete tower features three distinct sections: a base, shaft, and ornamental cap. The building is faced with brick, terracotta, and brick veneer. In addition to its decorative cap, which features coupled corbel and bracket cornice, the building is crowned by an eye-catching oval-electric sign. Formerly a Coca-Cola sign, the 58-foot tall sign now displays the logo of the defunct Western Automotive Parts Company. Developers bought the local landmark in 1999 and converted it into loft condominiums.

Longfellow Neighborhood Commercial Buildings

2506-2512 Holmes Street
1912-1915

Builders:
Marshall Brothers (2506-08)
Claud H. Lewis (2510)
Ora V. Thomas (2512)

Corbelling and patterned brickwork embellish these two-story tapestry brick buildings, located on "Dutch Hill" in what was an early 20th century German community. These buildings, including 2500-2504 Holmes, combined the convenience of second-floor living quarters with street-level stores.

Longfellow Residences

2900-2914 Campbell Street
1893-1896

Creating an exceptionally imposing panorama are these three-story houses of diverse architectural designs. The styles include: an Italianate Revival design at 2900 Campbell; an amalgam design of Queen Anne and Neoclassical elements at 2906 Campbell (architect: Walter C. Root); a modest version of the Queen Anne style at 2910 Campbell; and another house influenced by the Neoclassical and Chicago School at 2914 Campbell.

Union Hill Residences

3000-3017 DeGroff Way
1898-1899

Developer:
William Rockhill Nelson

These houses, similar in design, represent a subdivision planned and developed by William Rockhill Nelson, owner of The Kansas City Star, and reflect his belief that even the smallest houses should be planned with some degree of architectural skill.

Nelson's first attempt at this form of development was a row of small houses on the south side of 31st Street between Walnut Street and Grand Avenue. DeGroff Way, named for Nelson's father Isaac DeGroff Nelson, was his second venture. The idea was to show how a side street with inexpensive houses could be attractive; part of Nelson's solution here was to build only on alternate lots, landscaping the intervening space.

Among the early occupants was John Van Brunt, a distinguished Kansas City architect who lived at 3001 DeGroff Way.

J.W. Axtell Residence

2937 Walnut Street
1897; add. 1983

The intricate Eastlake style porch is the dominant feature of this Victorian residence. Its turned posts, spindles, and dainty brackets embellish the otherwise severe structure.

The Eastlake style is named for Charles Lock Eastlake, an English architect whose buildings include San Francisco row houses of the 1880s.

Union Cemetery

Warwick Trafficway at 28th Terrace
1856; add. c. 1903

This peaceful 33-acre tract of grass and trees stands
serene and quiet in the heart of the city and contains
the graves of thousands of Kansas Citians, some whose
names survive and others who lie in unmarked anonym-
ity. Although Union and Confederate soldiers are buried
here, the cemetery does not take its name from the
Civil War but from the fact that the cemetery was established through the united efforts of the City of Kansas
and Westport. Among the historically significant people
buried here is George Caleb Bingham, Missouri's most
famous 19th century artist.

Liberty Memorial

100 West 26th Street
1923-1926

Architect:
H. Van Buren Magonigle,
New York

Builder:
Westlake Construction Co.,
St. Louis

Situated on Memorial Hill, this reinforced concrete structure, sheathed in cut limestone, consists of two wings adjoined to a 217-foot tower. The plan for the Memorial (dedicated to the World War I dead), was selected through a national competition. Magonigle's design was the unanimous choice.

In 1921, the dedication of the ground was held before an estimated crowd of 100,000 people. Five of the commanders of the Allied Forces attended, including General John J. Pershing. In 1926, President Calvin Coolidge officially dedicated the memorial.

Sweeney Auto School

18

215 West Pershing
1916-1917

Architect:
Keene & Simpson

Builder:
George M. Bliss Construction Co.

Emory J. Sweeney, an automobile and tractor educator, contracted with local architectural firm Keene & Simpson to design a massive, 10-story brick building to house his growing trade school. Those involved with the project designed the building so that it could be converted into a hotel if the school faltered. Sweeney used his new building's height to his advantage, installing radio broadcasting antennas and large signs on the roof. The massive trade school closed in 1929, but the West Pershing Building was not converted into a hotel. Instead, the Business Men's Assurance Company of America (BMA), a Kansas City insurance company, purchased the building and converted it into office space. The new tenants installed a large fixture capable of producing multicolored light. Using the "BMA Beacon," the company offered a color-coded weather forecast: green light meant fair weather; orange signaled clouds; orange flashing predicted rain; and white flashing foretold snow. BMA left the building in 1963 and the building, renovated in 2003, is now known as the Pershing Building.

U.S. Post Office

315 West Pershing Road
1930-1933

Architect:
J.A. Wetmore,
Washington, D.C.

Builder:
Ring Construction Co.

A massive federal structure from an era of massive spending, the former United States Post Office is a behemoth designed by James A. Wetmore, the then-acting supervisor for the United States Treasury Department. The colonnaded Neoclassical Revival structure required three years and $4,000,000 to complete, and featured steel and concrete construction clad in limestone. The location at Broadway and Pershing took advantage of the rail access at nearby Union Station. In 1936, the Pershing facility was the third busiest in the nation, trailing only Chicago and New York in total volume. The pace would not hold, however, as airmail supplanted trains as the Postal Service's primary carrier in 1963, and the structure became underused. In 2004 the Internal Revenue Service agreed to an adaptive reuse plan centered on renovating and expanding the former Post Office into an IRS Service Center. Dedicated in 2006, the new facility brought an estimated 4,000 permanent and 2,000 seasonal jobs to downtown Kansas City, while the remaining postal operations relocated to nearby Union Station.

Penn Valley Park

Pershing Road & Main Street
1900-1926

Landscape Architect:
George E. Kessler

Penn Valley Park, one of the earliest in the city, was chosen for development largely because its rugged natural setting appealed to Kessler, who was commissioned in 1892 to provide an overall park plan for the city. The 176-acre park, in a sense, was the city's first urban

renewal project. It covers an area once dotted with unpainted shacks, threaded with dirt paths and known as "Vinegar Hill." Several famous Kansas City landmarks lie within its boundaries, including The Indian Scout. Sculpted by Cyrus E. Dallin, this statue won a gold medal at San Francisco's 1915 exposition.

Penn Valley Park Maintenance Building

3001 Central Street
1909-1910

Architect:
Root & Siemens

Builder:
Alexander Kinghorn

Displaying exceptional masonry work, this English Revival style structure was originally built as a stable and storage barn for the Parks Department. Featured in this building are towers, turrets, round-arched apertures, and chimney stacks.

J.B. Fugate Residence

3140 Coleman Road
1913

Architect:
Boillot & Lauck

Builder:
Swofford Realty Co.

This two-story stucco and wood frame residence is distinguished by a gable that extends to the first story. It was built as part of the Coleman Heights neighborhood, developed by the Swofford Realty Company. This neighborhood was part of a 180-acre farm purchased by residential developer James J. Swofford, who in 1914 began developing the Eastwood Hills addition.

Clarence W. Sondern Residence

3600 Belleview Avenue
1940; add. 1950

Architect:
Frank Lloyd Wright, Chicago

Situated on a bluff overlooking Roanoke Park, this low-setting residence is an example of domestic architecture that Wright personally developed and termed Usonian. This style is characterized by concrete slab flooring containing steam pipes, which provide radiant heating, and masonry core walls sandwiched by laminated wood panels.

The residence was built for Dr. Clarence W. Sondern, laboratory director of George A. Breon and Company. Under the ownership of Arnold Adler, the structure's original L-shaped plan, typical of Usonian homes, was changed to a composite T-shape by a living room addition.

Thomas Hart Benton Residence 24

3616 Belleview Avenue

1903-1904

Architect:
George A. Mathews

Located directly south of the Frank Lloyd Wright-designed Sondern Residence is this two-and-a-half-story stone masonry, Neoclassical style residence. It was built for Walter E. Kirkpatrick, secretary and treasurer of the Kansas City Electric Light Company. In 1939 the residence became the home of artist Thomas Hart Benton. The rear carriage house served as Benton's studio.

Following the death of Thomas and Rita Benton in 1975, the State of Missouri acquired the property with plans to maintain the house as a state historic site.

Joseph H. Rush Residence

3712 Madison Street
1902

This handsome Georgian Revival style residence was built for Joseph H. Rush, general agent for the Fidelity and Casualty Company of New York. The two-and-a-half-story buff brick structure is embellished by a decorative central bay of ornate classical detail. The house is part of the Roanoke residential district, an area situated on land that once served as the Kansas City Interstate Fairgrounds. The fairgrounds, which included a race track, ran from 38th Street and Pennsylvania Avenue west to Roanoke Road and north to Valentine Road.

Norman Tromanhauser Residence 26

3603 West Roanoke Drive
1914-1915

Architect: Builder:
Louis S. Curtiss   Brown & Johnson

One of Kansas City's best-known architects, Louis
S. Curtiss, planned this residence for his friends, the
Tromanhausers. A personal interpretation of the Prairie
School style, it is one of the last houses designed by
Curtiss. To his biographers, Curtiss remained an enig-
matic figure. Said one: "Louis Curtiss is vaguely remembered as a strange and eccentric man of exceptional tal-
ent; one who combined unusual originality with a strange
feeling for traditional styles."

Willard G. Kenerson Residence 27

3601 State Line Road
1895

A charming example of the Queen Anne style, popular
in the 1890s, is this asymmetrical wood frame residence
built for Willard G. Kenerson, a contractor and carpenter.
Especially pleasing is the ornate Eastlake front porch
with its turned posts and spindles. The house is situated
on a hill above a stone retaining wall.

William Volker Residence

3717 Bell Street
c. 1889

Architect:
Shepard & Farrar

More commonly known as "Roselawn," this three-story brick and shingle house is representative of the Shingle style, but is less noted for its architecture than for its longtime resident, William Volker, philanthropist and multimillionaire. Emigrating from Germany, Volker came to Kansas City in 1882 and in about 1890 purchased the house from Walter G. Mellier, who had built it for his residence in the late 1880s. Nicknamed "Mr.

Anonymous of Bell Street," Volker devoted a large share of his profits from a successful home furnishing business to local welfare, educational, and medical facilities.

Roanoke United Methodist Church 29
1717 West 41st Street
1921

The main façade (north) features three entrances – two entrances are in the dominant full gable and consist of paired doors with transoms. Cut stone and brick panels decorate the gable as does a cut stone parapet. Another entrance is located in a projecting bay at the eastern end of the main façade. Rectangular windows with tracery and stone sills run along the main façade.

Roanoke Presbyterian Church

1617 West 42nd Street
1930

Architect:
Felt, Dunham & Kriehn

Builder:
J.E. Crosby

An excellent example of Tudor Revival, construction of Roanoke Presbyterian Church was completed in 1931 at a cost of $125,000. Noteworthy features of the church include a side-placement crenelated belfry; paired glass panel door within a Tudor arch with cut stone quoin surrounds; cut stone and brick string coursing on the tower; and brick buttresses.

Swedish Evangelical Mission Church

1501 West 42nd Street
1912

Architect:
Ernest O. Brostrom

This modest red brick church, nestled in a residential
area between Westport and the state line, originally
served the neighborhood's Swedish Lutheran population. Tudor-style depressed arches filled with art glass
windows decorate the church's eastern and northern
façades. White paneling descends from the roof and
meets the arch in each fenestration. The superstructure
rests on a rusticated gray stone base, and the exterior
surfaces are largely unadorned, save for stone buttresses and an embattled parapet that surrounds the tower.
With an intersecting gable roof and side-tower floor plan,
the church originally lacked a parish house or rectory. A
two-story addition, built on the western elevation in 1949,
solved this problem by creating more space for church
meetings and housing for clergy. The addition seamlessly integrates with the style of the pre-existing structure.

Emil Rohrer Residence

4425 Terrace Street
1938

Architect:
Philip T. Drotts

Builder:
Richard L. Webb

The Moderne or Bauhaus feeling of stark, cubic simplicity predominates in this two-story residence built for Rohrer, a cement contractor. To comply with the owner's desire for a fireproof home, the architect chose an exterior construction of concrete blocks faced with stucco and an interior finish of insulating plaster. Floors are concrete slabs supported by precast concrete joists. Even the roof, made of fire resistant materials, is placed on concrete joists.

Heider-James Residence

4212 Washington Street
1896

Builder:
Martin Heider

The Heider-James Residence is a good example of a house related to the African-American enclave in Steptoe. It was built by German immigrant Martin Heider and subsequently bought by Arthur and Beatrice James. Arthur James was the second-ever African-American master plumber in Kansas City and is representative of the population of the community of Steptoe, an antebellum African-American neighborhood in the historic Westport district. Residents of Steptoe once declared their community "the best colored neighborhood in the city."

Some of Westport's most prominent citizens owned slaves, including John Calvin McCoy and John Wornall. McCoy established a method for slaves in the Westport area to buy their freedom. Slaves could earn $3 per week to work off repaying the price their masters had paid for them. This, coupled with the fact that the found-

St. James Baptist Church

508 West 43rd Street
1938; 1988 reconstruction

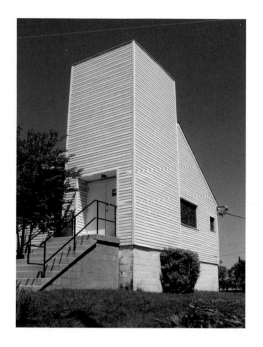

ing families of Westport set aside land for former slaves to live, makes this a unique chapter in the city's history.

In its time, Steptoe was considered "a little island" surrounded by white neighborhoods. Longtime residents talk about having white, Jewish, German, Italian, Hispanic, and Swedish neighbors. Though there were segregationist attitudes, there was little racial tension. Institutions were created to serve the local African-American population, including St. James Baptist Church – one of two churches that were located in the area for the African-American residents. St. Luke's was demolished in 2003 and St. James is the only remaining institution remaining in the Steptoe neighborhood.

Albert G. Boone's Store

500 Westport Road
1850-1851; adds. 1880-1882, 1894-1904

Situated in the commercial heart of historic Westport, Boone's Store stands as a focal point of the growth and development of this once thriving 19th century Missouri pioneer town. Erected during the height of the overland freighting industry, its early proprietor was Albert Gallatin Boone, grandson of Daniel Boone. The store built a thriving business by serving the many travelers along the Santa Fe and Oregon Trails. Other early buildings in the old town of Westport include the Jim Bridger Store, 504 Westport Road, and Mabry Hall, 4112-4114 Pennsylvania Avenue.

Westport United Methodist Church

500 West 40th Street
1897; adds. 1917, 1925

Architect:
Root & Siemens

The Westport Methodist Church congregation dates
back to 1826, but the current church building was constructed almost one hundred years later. The church
complex consists of sanctuary, bell tower, and substantial four-story parish house. The sanctuary's base is clad
in rusticated stone, likewise the bell tower and parish
house base. The sanctuary has an intersecting gable
roof, which connects to the window lintel via a shingled
face that features several louvered lancet vents. A
large, rounded arch window with art glass decorates the
sanctuary. The church follows the side-tower floor plan; a
pyramid-roofed belvedere crowns the adjoining bellower.
The large parish house is faced with stucco and features
a parallel double-gable roof. One of the roof segments
has a bank of dormer-shed windows. Altogether, the
church blends several surface textures – stucco, rusticated stone, and shingles – to create a unique style.

Our Lady of Good Counsel Church 37

3932 Washington Street
1906

Architecturally, Our Lady of Good Counsel is a fine
example of the neo-Palladian style, including an empha-
sis on symmetry, proportion, and reference to classical
temple styles. Its symmetrical features – including twin
domed towers, window bays mirroring entrances, and
classical gable pediment with oculus – all faithfully follow
Palladio's dictates.

The Our Lady of Good Counsel congregation originally
worshiped in smaller buildings that predate the current
1906 structure. After the church was completed, the
Sisters of Loretto converted one of the former church
buildings into a parish school. The diocese closed the
parish school as part of an educational restructuring
plan in 1969 and dedicated the parish to serve its elderly
members. In 2006, Bishop Finn declared the church the
diocesan Shrine to the Divine Mercy and St. Faustina.

Broadway Baptist Church

3931 Washington Street
1922

Architect:
Philip T. Drotts

The congregation must have had confidence in architect Phillip Drotts as he was not only a member of the church, but also a deacon. His large Norman Revival design features coursed stone walls and gothic windows with extensive tracery. The main, eastern façade rises to a gable point. The nave walls have three bays of windows; each consists of many lancet windows, similar to the front façade. The roof has three louvered gable dormers on each side, and alarge shed dormer with three windows over the northern rear entrance. The rear-mounted parish house is something of a surprise. Its basement and first floor are made of the same stone as the rest of the church, but the third and fourth floors are clad in Tudor Revival style, faced with beige stucco and turquoise half-timbers. Originally known as the Scandinavian Baptist Church, the Sunday sermon rang out in Swedish – but only until 1924.

Rev. Nathan Scarritt Residence 39

4038 Central Street
1847; reno. 1970

Builder:
Joseph O. Boggs

This antebellum frame house is believed to be the oldest residence in the Westport area. It was built about 1847 by Joseph O. Boggs and sold to Rev. Nathan Scarritt, a Methodist minister, in the 1850s. Scarritt came to Westport in 1852 to teach at the Shawnee Mission Indian Training School. He was one of the builders, as well as an early principal, of Westport High School.

The house is a two-story L-shaped building with an open porch on the south facade and retains the original window glass.

John Harris Residence

40

4000 Baltimore Street
1885; add. 1870

This fine brick antebellum home, designed in a Greek Revival style, was erected by early pioneer, Colonel John Harris. Harris was proprietor of Westport's most popular hostelry, the Harris House Hotel. The Harris residence originally stood near the intersection of Westport Road and Main Street. In the early 1920s, a severe preservation crisis occurred, due to the changing character of the neighborhood. In 1922, the Harris Home Association acquired the house and moved it to its present location.

First Calvary Baptist Church

3921 Baltimore
1890; adds. 1940,1950,1960

Architect:
Willis Polk; Joseph W.
Radotinsky; Stephen Kinney

Builder:
A. Sutermeister,
Bennett Construction Co.

Some of the most iconic names in Kansas City history helped build First Clavary Baptist Church: J. B. Wornall donated the parcel of land in 1886; a member of the congregation – W.W. Polk – designed the church; Wornall and Seth Ward contributed to the first capital campaign. Founded as the Westport Baptist Church, the new church was dedicated in 1889, and in 1922, the congregation merged with Cavalry Baptist Church and adopted the name First Calvary Baptist Church.

The church building itself has undergone several major changes. The main northern sanctuary, a rusticated stone structure with pilasters and Romanesque windows, has lost its former steeple. A chapel was built on the southern end of the lot in 1950. A modernist brick addition, added in 1960, connects the original sanctuary to the chapel.

St. Paul Episcopal Church

11 E 40th Street
1905

Architect:
William Barnes Fall

St. Paul's simple gable roof structure and restrained Norman style belies delicate, subtle artisanship. Van Brunt & Howe prepared the initial design in 1902, but it was English-born architect William Barnes Fall who submitted the final plans for the sanctuary. Featuring Gothic arched windows, mildly coursed ashlar stone, and a 65-foot embattled tower, the church makes good use of limited embellishment. The louvered lancet gable vent, the small Celtic cross adorning the roof peak, and the crenellated narthex maintain visual interest while affecting a simple, refined style.

The interior provides similar conservative design while celebrating a remarkable collection of art glass. The dark wood exposed trusses and ceiling push the visitor's attention to the nave's stained glass. Not a part of the original design, the first stained glass window was installed in 1922. The collection features works by Jacoby Art Glass of St. Louis, Willet Studio of Philadelphia, and the Powell and Sons/Whitefriars Glassworks of Great Britain. In addition to the sanctuary, several other structures populate the St. Paul's campus – many serve the church's eponymous primary school, which opened in 1963.

Third Church of Christ, Scientist

3953 Walnut Street
1913; altered 1921-22

Architect:
Keene & Simpson

Builder:
Bert L. Elmer, contractor
Long Construction Co.

This is a church built in two phases. The congregation purchased the land in 1911. The congregation requested the architects design a church with a basement and grand auditorium, with the intention to build and occupy the basement before even beginning construction on the main hall. The basement was completed in 1913, and the congregation held services there. Construction on the church superstructure was completed in 1922, but the building was not dedicated until 1926, when the debt was discharged. Christian Science churches, as a matter of denominational fiat, are not dedicated until debt free.

The church building features Neoclassical design elements. The main façade has three main entrance doors interspersed between four Ionic columns. Each doorway has a stone pediment over the lintel, and a Romanesque arched window above the pediment. The brick walled structure rests on a white ashlar stone base. Three bays of round-arched art glass windows decorate the nave, and a bracketed cornice and parapet crown the church.

Westport High School

315 East 39th Street
1907-1908; addition 1964-1965

Architect:
Charles A. Smith

Builder:
Swenson Construction

This massive brick building, completed in 1908, was hailed as "the finest school in Kansas City and among the finest in the whole country." Smith designed more than 50 buildings for the Kansas City school district.

During the Civil War, the school was disbanded but it was reestablished in 1867 on the site of the present Allen Elementary School. The present building replaced a structure at 39th and Warwick Boulevard that was destroyed by fire in 1907.

Gillham Park Maintenance Bldg.   45
39th Street & Gillham Road
1905

Architects:
Adriance Van Brunt & Brother

Constructed in 1905, the structures were originally designed to accommodate the sizable human and equestrian workforce necessary to maintain Kansas City's growing network of parks and scenic boulevards. The main, two-story square building features a hip roof and a segmental through-the-cornice dormer window on the main façade. The walls are rusticated stone, while the bays are edged with enclosed red brick. Likewise, red brick also encloses the large main entrance. There are two adjoining stable structures, each made with the same rusticated stone and hip roof.

The Gillham Park Maintenance Building and accompanying stables became victims of both time and technological change. Horses are no longer a necessary part of park maintenance, and parks no longer need individual maintenance buildings. The building's historic connection to the original Kessler park system, combined with the low survival rate for service buildings, make preserving the Gillham Park Maintenance Building important for Kansas City's historic architectural diversity.

William C. Schmidt Residence

4049 McGee Street
1896

Leaded art glass of superior quality distinguishes this charming one-and-a half-story Queen Anne style cottage, built for William C. Schmidt, whom the 1897 Hoye's City Directory simply describes as a "driver." The asymmetrical design carried out in a wood frame construction exemplifies similar cottages within the immediate area.

George C. Wright Residence

4315 Warwick Boulevard
1907-1908

Architect:
Albert Turney

Neoclassical elements embellish this Prairie School style residence of cut stone and brick painted white. A porte-cochere extends from the north facade. A carriage house to the east matches the main building. The house was built for George G. Wright, who came to Kansas City in 1906 and established a land-dealing business that extended to Minnesota, North Dakota, Canada, Texas, and Mexico.

The Zurn Colonnades

48

301-319 East 43rd Street
1922

Builder:
Zurn Building & Investment Co.

These eleven classically designed brick apartment buildings, whose three-story Corinthian columns form an impressive colonnade along East 43rd Street, supplanted a turn-of-the-century estate. The stone wall surrounding the apartments is the original wall built around the twenty-room stone residence of businessman and banker, William Ashley Rule. The mansion was razed in 1930. Apartments of this type are characteristic of many Kansas City neighborhoods.

R.E. Bruner Residence - Mineral Hall

4340 Oak Street
1903-1904; add.1905

Architect:
Louis S. Curtiss

Builder:
Henry H. Johnson

An impressive, semi-circular, compound arched main entrance, composed of imported mosaics and leaded art glass, makes Mineral Hall one of the most distinctive turn-of-the-century residences in Kansas City. Most noticeably influenced by the Art Nouveau movement, other artistic influences in its design include Prairie School, Second Empire, and Neoclassical styles. Mineral Hall derived its name from its first owner, Roland E. Bruner, a mining tycoon, whose magnificent mineral collection of some 10,000 specimens was partly housed in the north addition.

August R. Meyer Residence

50

4415 Warwick Boulevard
1896-1897, add. 1929

Architects:
Van Brunt & Howe; Wight & Wight (1929)

This 26-room, red brick, Flemish Queen Anne style mansion, formerly known as "Marburg," was owned by August R. Meyer, president of the consolidated Kansas City Smelting and Refining Company and first president of the Kansas City Park Board.

Acquisition of the A.R. Meyer residence and a tract of eight and a half acres of nearby land in 1928 provided the Kansas City Art Institute with a home. This was made possible by Howard S. Vanderslice, one of Kansas City's outstanding philanthropists and art patrons. Known today as Vanderslice Hall, this structure houses the administration offices of the Art Institute.

Nelson-Atkins Museum of Art

4525 Oak Street
1930-1933

Architect:
Wight & Wight

Builder: Long Construction Co.

Made possible by the bequests of William Rockhill Nelson; his widow, Ida Houston Nelson; his daughter and son-in-law, Mr. and Mrs. Irwin Kirkwood; and Mrs. Mary F. Atkins, the Nelson Gallery-Atkins Museum stands today in place of "Oak Hall." Nelson's residence was razed for the purpose of erecting a suitable structure to house and exhibit the art collections his generosity brought to Kansas City.

Designed in a Neoclassical Revival style, the exterior walls are sheathed in Indiana limestone ornamented with twenty-three sculptured panels in low relief. The panels, designed by Charles Keck, depict the exploration and settlement of the Middle West.

The aesthetic treatment evidenced within the twenty acres of surrounding grounds was designed by the

Landscape Architects:
Hare & Hare

landscape architectural firm of Hare and Hare, and was
included in the approximate building cost of $2,750,000.

Rockhill Neighborhood

46th Street to Pierce Street,
Locust Street to Troost Avenue
1901-1910

The Rockhill Neighborhood was planned and developed by William Rockhill Nelson, publisher of The Kansas City Star. A former building contractor, Nelson pursued his interests in architecture and urban design long after becoming a newspaper publisher. His design for the Rockhill district with its modest but tasteful houses is considered a physical expression of his concept of the City Beautiful movement, which he promoted in news stories and editorials, as well as in stone and concrete.

This neighborhood was developed on property Nelson acquired about 1890. Certain larger homes in the district, such as 704 East 47th Street, were built for speculation, but most of the smaller dwellings were rental properties, some intended for use by his employees.

Nelson's houses are characterized by frame construction with clapboard or shingle siding and locally quarried limestone. The homes are of identical or similar design within each block, but each block is different. In addition,

the homes on 47th Terrace, Pierce Street, and Harrison Street are placed on only one side of the street, allowing each residence an unobstructed view.

An important feature of the neighborhood is Rockhill Road, which exemplifies Nelson's belief in the practicality of contoured boulevards as aspects of proper urban residential design.

United Bretheren Church

4000 Harrison Street
1907

Builder:
Clark Williams Construction

This red brick, side-steeple church features an uncommon combination of architectural features. White, Gothic limestone relieving arch lintels accent the window bays along the main façade and throughout the design. According to the original plans, the designers intended the circular openings in the side-steeple to house a clock, and the top of the tower featured crenellation. The crenelated motif would have matched the Gothic arched windows, perhaps pushing the design further towards Gothic Revival than its current fusion style. In 1922, the church was remodeled, adding a second floor to the education building. The first congregation of United Brethren in Kansas City initially occupied the building. (The Brethren were originally a circuit-riding, orthodox evangelical Christian movement.)

St. Mark Lutheran Church

3800 Troost Avenue
1914, add. 1924

Architect:
Owen & Payson (stone church)
Shepard & Wiser (Tudor addition)

Builder:
Charles W. Lovitt

This two-story Gothic Revival Church and attached
Tudor-style parsonage and parish house dominate the
streetscape. The church's exterior is clad in rusticated
stone, and a massive, Gothic arched art glass window
decorates the church's main façade. Two towers flank
the arched art-glass window; the right tower features a
louvered belfry. Five bays of large, Gothic arched art-
glass windows continue down the length of the nave.
The building then transitions into Tudor style. A rusticated stone base supports beige stucco walls with dark
brown trim and half-timbers. The three-story parish
house and parsonage feature a complex roof. The
parsonage roof, like the church, is slate covered and
gabled. The roof culminates with a half-hip gable roof at
the western elevation. This church's design successfully
fuses the Gothic and Tudor styles.

The Hyde Park neighborhood features a potpourri of popular turn-of-the-century single family residential architectural styles. Construction began at the end of the 19th century and largely ceased by 1920. Designed for Kansas City's affluent citizens, typical houses in Hyde Park display high levels of design quality and craftsmanship. The neighborhood contains examples of popular national styles, including Colonial Revival, Shingle style, Queen Anne, Victorian Romanesque, and the Prairie School Style. In addition, Hyde Park also features a large number of popular local vernacular styles, like the Kansas City "Shirtwaist."

Prominent citizens flocked to the segregated area, drawn by the quality homes and prestige associated with a Hyde Park address. Notable residents included the local architect Henry Van Brunt, railroad magnate Arthur Stilwell, and former Missouri Governor Herbert Hadley. In addition to the fine homes, residents also had exclusive access to the adjacent Hyde Park. Designed by noted landscape architect George Kessler, Hyde Park was a "proof of concept" development. Its success encouraged city officials, and as a result, the Park Board empowered Kessler to design and implement his City Beautiful plan for Kansas City.

James H. Harkless Residence

3600 Harrison Street
1905

Typifying many fine homes in Hyde Park, this exquisite Mission style residence is distinguished by its rough hewn stone walls and cut stone coping, as well as its arched, main entrance porch. A carriage house of near identical design is placed to the rear.

Harkless, a prominent attorney, not only served as president of the Kansas City Bar Association and the Missouri Bar, but was an active participant in the Kansas City Chapter of the American Red Cross.

Central Presbyterian Church 58

901 East Armour Boulevard
1924

Architect:
Shepard & Wiser

With its Ionic columns and unadorned pediment, the
Central Presbyterian Church's primary façade is a striking, stark example of the Neoclassical architectural style.
Though the entablature is engraved with the church's
name, the façade offers few clues as to the building's
purpose – no crosses or other religious icons. The
congregation traces its roots back to fourteen founding
members that chartered the church in 1857. Originally,
the members worshipped at a pair of downtown locations, but decided to relocate to a single location in
Hyde Park. Designed in 1920 and completed in 1924,
the building has survived largely unaltered through the
intervening decades. The façade rests on a white stone
base, and that same white stone accents the buff brick
walls, both as quoining and surrounding the window
bays. Multi-level art glass decorates the nave's curved-
arch Romanesque windows. A brick parapet surrounds
the church's flat roof.

Charles Granniss Residence

720 East 36th Street
1906

Architect:
John McKecknie

This handsome brick and cut stone residence is a unique example of the Arts and Crafts design, an American interpretation of the Art Nouveau movement during the early 20th century. It was built for Charles E. Granniss, president of the Pineland Manufacturing Company.

at East 36th Street

Janssen Place is one of the earliest examples of turn-of-the-century, planned residential development in the city. Richly landscaped and set in a profusion of shade trees and ornamental shrubbery, the homes here still project an aura of opulence that was the intention of their developer 75 years ago. Janssen Place was conceived in 1897 by Arthur E. Stilwell, railroad magnate, who intended to create a residential layout plan with a grand ornamental Neoclassical gateway. The development is named for August Janssen, Dutch capitalist and a friend of Stilwell. Janssen Place became known as "Lumber-man's Row" because many of the early home owners were associated with the lumber industry.

The district is divided into 32 lots facing a broad private boulevard. The homes reflect a variety of architectural designs including: Italianate Revival, Shingle, Queen Anne, Georgian Revival, and Jacobethan Revival styles.

Notre Dame de Sion School

3823 Locust Street
1927

Architect:
Wilkinson & Crans

This four-story buff brick and frame school building overlooks nearby Gillham Park. Originally designed to accommodate two hundred students, the school notably featured a laboratory, library, gymnasium, and swimming pool. A Spanish-style parapet crowns the primary southern façade, and bays of round arched lancet windows dominate the western elevation. Formerly run by the Sisters of Our Lady of Sion, a French Catholic Order, the campus currently offers coeducational classes for students up to middle school age; older female students attend the high school campus, which opened in South Kansas City in 1961.

Apartment Buildings on Armour   62

Armour Boulevard between Broadway & Paseo
1902-1930

The majority of the extant structures along Armour Boulevard are apartments and hotels. These structures were erected during two distinct time periods: 1902-1910 and 1911-1930. The very prominent Kansas City architect, John W. McKecknie, designed a series of apartments during this period which are located on the north and south sides of Armour Boulevard between Wyandotte and Baltimore streets. Another outstanding apartment building constructed on Armour Boulevard during this early period was the Chalfonte Apartments, 1110 East Armour Boulevard, a fine example of the Classical Revival style of architecture.

Many impressive apartment/hotel buildings were constructed during the second time period (1911-30). They are designed in a variety of architectural styles including Italianate, Tapestry Brick, Gothic Revival, Sullivanesque, Jacobethan, Neoclassical, and the Arts and Craft Movement. Many prominent Kansas City architects such as Nelle E. Peters, Walter Besecke, and John Braecklein designed these imposing structures.

Newbern Apartments

525 East Armour Boulevard
1921-1923; add. 1925

Architect:
Brostrom & Drotts

Builder:
Harold A. Noble, consulting engineer

The Newbern Apartments are only one example of the fine construction that occurred in the first part of the 20th century on Armour Boulevard, once one of the more fashionable boulevards in the city.

Nearly identical, these two nine-story buildings are constructed of reinforced concrete with exteriors of brick and Sullivanesque style terra cotta. Known as The Peacock for several years after opening, the apartments were bought by Berne H. Hopkins, who changed the name and added the connecting unit that now serves as the main entrance.

William M. Reid Residence 64

300 East 36th Street
1907

Architect:
Root & Siemens

The Reid's Tudor Revival home was patterned after a very large English house built in Wiltshire in 1675. This brick house has a slate roof, gabled parapets, a limestone balustrade and nine chimneys.

William Magraw Reid was a realtor, builder, and a former director of the First National Bank. Mr. and Mrs. Reid traveled in Europe extensively, and many winters were spent in Paris and on the Riviera. On these travels antique furnishings were accumulated to reproduce the atmosphere of an English country house. He spent many years collecting furniture, lamps, wall hangings, and rugs, some woven to his specifications in Turkey. In December 1921, the mansion was sold with its furnishings to Dessa M. Skinner, general agent of the Aetna Insurance Company, for $70,000 and the Reids departed for Paris. The property was acquired in 1956 by the Kansas City-St. Joseph Catholic Diocese and a three-story Modern addition was built on the west side of the residence in 1959.

William B. Knight Residence

3534 Walnut Street
1890

Architect:
Adriance Van Brunt

Half-timbering marks the attic level of this three-story brick residence, an example of the 19th century Stick style that is vaguely reminiscent of both Swiss chalet and English forms.

The house was built for William Baker Knight, a nationally renowned civil engineer who designed and constructed several of Kansas City's cable railway lines.

Westminster Congregational Church

3600 Walnut Street
1904

Architects:
Diboll & Owen;
Braecklein & Martling

Builder:
Louis Breitag

Built in the English Norman style, with rusticated stone walls, an embattled polygonal tower, and Tudor Arch windows, this squat-looking church has a militant presence. Carthage, Phoenix, and Blue Bedford limestone accents decorate the native blue limestone walls. The main entrance is at the Northwest elevation, through a gallery showcasing early-English capital columns. Large windows adorn the northern and western facades; delicate stone tracery cradles art glass by the Campbell Glass and Paint Company.

Westminster Congregational Church was originally built in 1904 according to the "Akron Plan," a popular church layout in the late 19th and early 20th centuries. Designed to maximize efficiency, the plan featured a central auditorium surrounded on all non-sanctuary sides by classrooms. The New Orleans architectural firm Diboll & Owen designed the 1904 Akron construction, with local Kansas City firm Martling & Braecklein acting as associate architects.

Longmeadow Historic District

1-7 East 34th Street
1888

This group of row houses is one of the last remaining examples of row homes built in the 1880s and 1890s when such blocks of multi-family residences were found in various styles and areas of the city. This masonry and wood building retains all the charm and exuberant details characteristic of the Eastlake and Queen Anne styles.

West Armour Apartments

100-118 West Armour Boulevard
1902-1903

68

Architect:
John McKecknie

Noted local architect John McKecknie designed these four Italianate apartment buildings for William H. Collins. The apartments represent a transitional period in residential construction on the scenic boulevard. These medium density low-rise structures – three duplexes and an 18-unit building once known as the "Collin's Flats" – are the early manifestations of an impulse that would lead later developers to construct large high rise apartment buildings.

McKecknie was a stylistic and functional pioneer. Noted for helping popularize Kansas City's now ubiquitous colonnade apartment style, McKecknie also pioneered the use of reinforced concrete in the late 19th and early 20th century. McKecknie was prolific and versatile. The Armour apartments display Italianate and Arts and Crafts Movement motifs; his other works heavily referenced Neoclassical and Egyptian Revival styles. Trained at Princeton and Columbia, McKecknie's oeuvre played an influential role in Kansas City's architectural history.

Knickerbocker Apartments

501-535 Knickerbocker Place
1909-1910

Architect:
Loren Grant Middaugh

Developer:
James Albert Rose

These venerable brick and stone apartments were once
one of the city's best apartment addresses after their
construction. The 56-unit group lines both sides of
Knickerbocker Place, a one-block street that was a
private thoroughfare. From 1910 to about 1925, they
comprised one of the largest apartment complexes in the
city. The north side was demolished in 1982.

Our Lady of Perpetual Help (Redemptorist Church)

3333 Broadway Boulevard
1907-1927

Architect:
Wilder & Wight

Builder:
Alexander King Co.

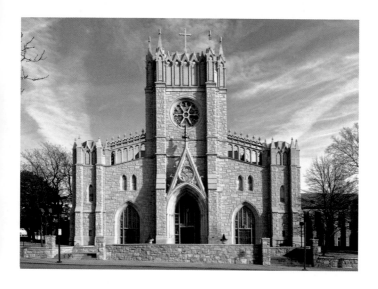

The construction of Our Lady of Perpetual Help, also known as the Redemptorist Church, the French Gothic church at the corner of Linwood and Broadway, was a massive undertaking. The church's ornate façade and expansive campus is a local landmark in Midtown.

Built from native limestone quarried at what would become Roanoke Park, the massive church features a rusticated façade, three Gothic-arched entrances, and an ornate balustrade parapet. A large rose window, with delicate tracery, adorns the bell tower. The nave extends east of the Broadway elevation, flanked by arcades to the north and south. The church's ribbed transverse arch ceilings, restored during renovations in 2000, soar over the pews. Two courses of stained glass – one in the clerestory, and another at ground level – decorate the nave.

**Country Club
Brookside
Waldo**

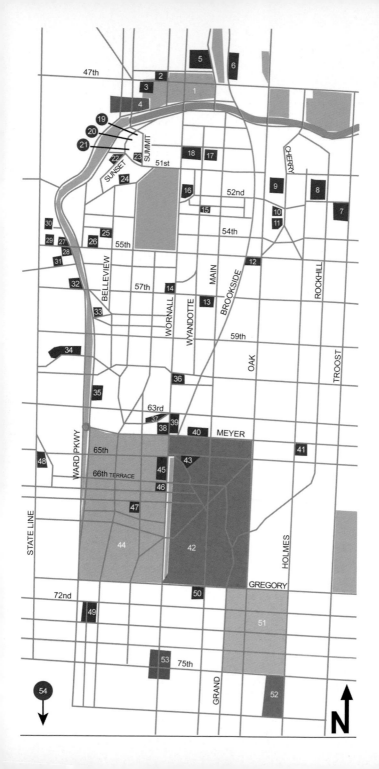

Country Club
Brookside
Waldo

Home to world class dining and shopping, the area known as the Country Club Plaza and surrounding Country Club District was once nothing more than an expanse of farmland and brushwood making it unsuitable for residential and leisurely purposes. Similarly, the now unique Waldo neighborhood was also once comprised of acres of farmland. Thanks in part to a doctor named David Waldo and J.C. Nichols, a real estate developer, the Waldo and Country Club Districts became unique communities nestled on the southern edge of Kansas City.

Located directly south of historic Westport, the Country Club District boasts a rich history. It has been traversed by the Santa Fe Trail and during the Civil War, served as the site of border conflict between Missouri and Kansas, as well as the fiercely fought Battle of Westport. At the end of the war the district was used primarily for farming and dairying, providing for the growing city to the north. The land remained like this until Nichols acquired it and began repurposing the land into a lovely residential community.

In 1907 the city limits ended at 47th Street, making the farmland that would later become the Country Club District a southern outlier to the city. Main Street was nothing but a narrow country lane and Oak Street was still a dirt road. In fact, there were no paved roads or utilities in the area. Moreover, Brush Creek coursed through dense low-lying marsh and added to the seemingly uninhabitable atmosphere of the land. The area as a whole seemed entirely dilapidated and certainly not prime real estate for Nichols' grand ideas.

Although a brilliant investment in retrospect, Nichols' venture to transform the undesirable land into gorgeous properties must have seemed speculative at the time.

In 1907 the wealthy continued to build mansions in the coveted Northeast district. Janssen Place and the surrounding Hyde Park area were in the midst of development, while Armour Boulevard, Troost Avenue, and The Paseo were already lined with elegant residences. It would prove difficult for Nichols to persuade homebuyers and builders to relocate to an undeveloped area like the Country Club District.

As Kansas City continued to develop it pushed further south from the Missouri and Kansas rivers, even past the bluffs. Perhaps recognizing a noticeable trend in Kansas City to continuously move south, J.C. Nichols purchased his first 10 acres at 51st and Grand Avenue in 1907. He began immediate construction on a small neighborhood and shopping center. As early as 1912, Nichols began to formulate plans for a more comprehensive business district in nearby Brush Creek valley. His goal was to create a buffer between the homes he was building on Sunset Hill and in Crestwood and the main business sector of the city. In choosing the name for the district, Nichols was inspired by the exclusive golf and country club that was then located at 55th Street and Wornall Road, now Loose Park. He appreciated the prestigious and affluent implications of the name, which would presumably attract the wealthy homebuilders of the time.

Before Nichol's plans for the Country Club District and surrounding area, the only thing linking the area to the Waldo District was a slow-moving steam train known as the "Dummy Line." The rail line connected Westport to Dobson, a small town in South Kansas City, and eventually the Country Club to Waldo. Streetcars later replaced the rail line in 1907 making the Country Club car line an essential source of transportation for Waldo residents. Even more importantly, the development of the Country

Club District made possible for more growth throughout the Waldo area. In 1909, just two years after J.C. Nichols began developing a small community in the Country Club District, Waldo was annexed by Kansas city making the city limits grow from 49th to 77th street. Just like the Country Club District, Waldo was originally a 1,000-acre tract of farmland that was purchased by Dr. David Waldo in1841. Waldo's land more than doubled in size and eventually became a charming, historic neighborhood that bore the doctor's name. Waldo, like the Country Club area, was seen as a retreat from crowded urban life and therefore made a perfect adjoining district. What makes Waldo so unique is that while it is a business district, more than 60 percent of the businesses are locally owned, adding to the close-knit community atmosphere. Today the district is regarded as a town within a city in which lies small businesses and family-oriented neighborhoods.

Although the Waldo District was already established, it continued to expand alongside the development of Nichol's dream community that would incorporate tree-lined boulevards and landscaped parkways. Intending to build up the area while following the natural terrain, Nichols employed the talents of George E. Kessler, designer of Kansas City's Parks and Boulevard System. Nichols' plan for the district was to create subdivisions that included residences, shops, schools, and churches. Seeking to maintain architectural harmony throughout all of these structures, he even built Tudor style fire and police stations and cut-stone streetcar-line shelters. The Country Club District encompasses numerous architectural styles favored in Kansas City. Colonial, Georgian, Tudor, and Italianate residences and buildings abound. It is this unique partnering of architecture styles that creates a neighborhood of distinction and has made it a desirable place to live for more than 80 years. Today the link between Waldo and the Country Club District is not as evident, as the two have grown into unique communities. Nevertheless, each shares the importance of extending the city limits and providing beautiful, historic communities that preserve sprawling neighborhoods and a family-like atmosphere amongst a bustling metropolis.

The Country Club Plaza

West 47th Street & Broadway
1922-present

Architect: Builder:
Edward Buehler Delk (1922-1925)   J.C. Nichols Co.
Edward W. Tanner (1925-1974)

The Country Club Plaza is synonymous with J.C.
Nichols. Simultaneously with his development of the
Country Club District, Nichols began thinking about an
"outlying business center," which would act as a gateway to his residential area. His eye fastened on a valley
between the hills bordering Brush Creek. Delk, architect
of the original plans for the area, carried out the Spanish theme, which Nichols felt would be both picturesque
and adaptable. Delk envisioned low buildings with red
tile roofs, wrought iron ornamentation and colorful towers. His earliest rendering shows a landscaped central
square; this was never constructed, but it provided the
name "Plaza."

No off-street parking was incorporated in the initial design, although several filling stations were among the early buildings erected on the Plaza, evidence that Nichols recognized the importance of the motorized customer. Within a few years, the Nichols Company was utilizing otherwise undeveloped tracts as landscaped parking facilities, a novel concept. Before J.C. Nichols, suburban shopping centers usually sprouted by chance; a planned development was virtually unknown.

The Plaza's architectural harmony, which is its most conspicuous feature, has brought it worldwide attention.

Seventh Church of Christ, Scientist

604 West 47th Street
1941

Architect:
G. Wilbur Foster

Builder:
Foster Engineering Co.

Planning for this church began in 1927 when Science
students met to discuss the establishment of a new
church in the Plaza area. The present building was constructed in 1941 at the cost of approximately $182,000.
The church unit consists of a church, Sunday school,
and a Christian Science Reading Room.

The church is a good example of Romanesque style
architecture and was designed by G. Wilbur Foster, an
architect from Indianapolis, Indiana.

Unity Temple

3

707 West 47th Street
1946

Architect:
Charles A. Smith

Builder:
Swenson Construction Co.

In February 1929, the Unity Society of Practical Christianity bought a $40,000 tract of land at the southwest corner of 47th and Jefferson streets. This was to be the site of its new temple. The building was designed by Smith in 1946 as a memorial to Myrtle Page Fillmore who, with her husband Charles Fillmore, founded the Unity School of Practical Christianity.

Above the main entry is a tripartite series of fenestration featuring art glass widows covered with decorative grill work and set in cast stone surrounds. A six-story bell tower reflects the similar-sized tower across the street at the Seventh Church of Christ, Scientist.

The Literary Apartments   4

700, 708, 712, 720 & 804 West 48th Street
4800 & 4804 Jefferson Street
4746 & 4809 Roanoke Parkway
1927-1929

Architect: Builder:
Nelle E. Peters   Charles E. Phillips

David Copperfield Apartments, 804 W. 48th Street

These apartment buildings at the western edge of the
Country Club Plaza are significant as distinguished
works of Nelle E. Peters. Peters was a prolific Kansas
City architect whose practice focused upon apartment
buildings and hotels. Peters' specific interest in apartment building design focused upon exterior treatment as
well as interior circulation.

The buildings in this thematic group are further significant for their association with Charles E. Phillips, a
prominent Kansas City builder/developer. Phillips and
Peters began working together in 1913 to design and
construct single family and small-scale apartment buildings. Phillips envisioned the area as a compact development which would house upwards of 1,000 families.

Cottesbrook Apartments, 708 W. 48th Street

The Literary Apartment buildings – named after historic writers and works of literature – reflect a sample of Nelle E. Peters' mature work and rely upon both historical reference and contemporary design. As a grouping, the apartment buildings present a unified urban streetscape that is enlivened by stylistic variety, paired facades, inter-related courtyards and similarity of materials.

Washington Irving Apartments, 4746 Roanoke Drive

Park Lane Apartments

5

4600 J.C. Nichols Parkway
1925-1926

Architect:
George B. Post & Sons,
New York

Builder:
Collins Brothers

The Park Lane Apartments is a six-story reinforced concrete and steel building featuring a brick and stone exterior. The irregular-shaped building with Mission Style elements was designed by the New York firm of George B. Post and Sons, and constructed in 1925-1926.

Post and Sons is credited with developing the modern hotel, and the Park Lane stands as one of the firm's notable designs. Its Mission Style design reflects the overall architectural vocabulary of the surrounding Country Club Plaza. Although the design of the building has been attributed to Alonzo H. Gentry, the actual plans list Gregory Vigeant as architect. At the time, both Vigeant and Gentry were employed by George B. Post and Sons. Gentry arrived in Kansas City in 1921 as a representative for the local office of Post and Sons and was present during the construction the structure.

Initially billed as a hotel/apartment complex, the units were priced for the moderate to upper income resident.

Community Christian Church

4601 Main Street
1940

Architects:
Frank Lloyd Wright
Edward Delk, supervising architect

Wright's original plan for the Community Christian Church had called for a light steel frame, flexible in shape, resting on a rock ballast foundation. The steel skeleton was to be covered by heavy paper strung with steel wires and then waterproofed with sprayed cement. This design created problems with the building codes and led to Wright's withdrawal from the project. The church was completed by Delk (within code requirements.)

The church features cantilevered balconies and low canopies, small fixed ribbon windows, five entrances on the main (north) façade, and a perforated concrete dome on the roof, which Wright used as the steeple.

In 1990, Artist Dale Eldred was commissioned to create a plan to fulfill Wright's original vision of "searchlights piercing the perforated masonry roof ... a steeple of light." The project was stalled by technology and Eldred's death until 1993 when Roberta Lord, Eldred's wife, completed the design and the "Steeple of Light" became a reality. A column of light is now projected skyward from the steeple each weekend, dusk to midnight.

001 East 52nd Street
1948-50

Architect: Builder:
Barry Byrne (Chicago)   C.A. Kelly
Joseph B. Shaughnessy, Sr.

Located near Rockhurst College, this steel and masonry edifice is revolutionary in both its concept and design. The church nave, conceived in the shape of a fish, represents an early liturgical symbol for Christ. Its elongated blue windows contrast dramatically with the stark whiteness of the cut limestone facades. The large 18-foot high sculpture of St. Francis Xavier, placed near the northeast entrances, was carved by Chicago sculptor, Alfonso Iannelli.

Walter S. Dickey Residence 8

5100 Rockhill Road
1912

Architect:
Roger Gilman; George B. Post &
Sons (NYC) consulting architect

Builder:
Charles C. Smith

A classic columned portico embellishes the front façade of this four-story limestone residence, built at a cost of $700,000. Assisting Kansas City architect Gilman was George B. Post of New York, designer of the New York Stock Exchange.

The house was built for Walter S. Dickey, president during the 1920s of the W. S. Dickey Clay Manufacturing Company and publisher of the now defunct Kansas City Journal Post.

Now called Scofield Hall, it is the University of Missouri-Kansas City's Administration Building.

Edwin W. Shields Residence 9

5110 Cherry Street
1909

Architects:
Wilder & Wight

Builder:
Nicholas Miller

This magnificent mansion of English Tudor design, known as "Oakland," was built for Edwin W. Shields, grain company president, and his wife, Martha, and named for the many native oak trees that grew on the undeveloped part of their property. The property also featured stables for horses and a small polo field.

Edwin Shields passed away in 1920, and Martha donated the vacant 10-acre tract of land on the south side of 52nd Street to her neighbor, the University of Kansas City. After Martha's death, the home and property passed through several hands, including Miss Barstow's School for Girls and the J.C. Nichols Real Estate Company.

In 1965, the University of Missouri Kansas City purchased the Shields Residence, and in 1973 the university bought the rest of the Shields property, including the former polo field at 52nd and Oak. The residence is now part of the Bloch School of Management.

U.S. Epperson Residence   **10**

5200 Cherry Street
1919-25

Architect:
Horace LaPierre

Uriah Spray Epperson was a wealthy underwriter of fire insurance for grain elevators and lumberyards. Construction of the Collegiate/Gothic style house began in 1919 and took six years to complete. The structure features half-timbering, a castellated tower and parapet walls, and dozens of diamond-paned leaded glass windows. Epperson lived in the 56-room home with his wife, Elizabeth, and Harriet Barse, a Kansas City Conservatory of Music student.

After the Eppersons' deaths, the home became the property of J.J. Lynn, a business associate of Epperson. Lynn had plans to use the property as offices for Epperson Underwriting Company but was met with opposition from affluent neighbors. Lynn instead donated the property to University of Missouri Kansas City (then called the University of Kansas City) in Sept. 1942.

During World War II, Epperson House was used to house aviation cadets.

Sen. James A. Reed Residence   **11**

5236 Cherry Street
1911-12

Architects:
Sanneman & Van Trump

Builder:
J.W. Mabry

This Georgian Revival style mansion, surrounded by
a handsome wrought iron fence and situated on tree-
shaded grounds, was built for Charles L. Merry, opti-
cian and jeweler. In 1921 it was purchased by James A.
O'Reilly, drug company president, but it is best known as
the home of James A. Reed, a three-term United States
Senator from Missouri.

James's wife, Nell Donnelly Reed, was as well-known
as her husband. She established the Donnelly Garment
Company with her then husband, Paul, in 1919. The
company was known for her designs and ready-to-wear
production method. By 1921 she had more than 1,000
employees. She is also known for her kidnapping by
three men in 1931 that held her for a $75,000 ransom
along with her chauffeur. It was a media sensation and
the kidnapper was acquitted because he stated that
once he realized he had kidnapped the wrong people,
he released them. She married Senator James Reed in
1933 after divorcing her husband the previous year.

Crestwood Shops

55th & Oak Street
1922

Architect:
Edward W. Tanner

Builder:
J.C. Nichols Co.

The Crestwood neighborhood, an early Nichols development, contains both retail stores and residences. The Nichols Company called the stores "Kansas City's first completely planned neighborhood center." The shops were designed in a vernacular Classic Revival style and were constructed of red brick with white wood trim.

The residential area east of the shops is forested with indigenous oaks and maples. The streets were laid out to take maximum advantage of the hilly terrain.

Judge H.F. McElroy Residence **13**

21 West 57th Street
1917

Builder:
Fred Liebe

This prairie style house was built in 1917. It was a popular style in the Country Club district. It features a hipped roof with dormers, stucco cladding and a unique gabled front portico.

This was the house of Henry F. McElroy, the city manager who had close ties to the "Boss" Tom Pendergast political machine. On May 27, 1933, his daughter, Mary McElroy, was kidnapped from here by four unknown criminals. The kidnappers received the ransom and released Mary at Milburn Golf club. The court handed down some of the harshest sentences for the time, including the death penalty for one kidnapper. Mary had befriended her kidnappers and would regularly visit them in prison.

Country Club United Methodist Church

400 West 57th Street
1922-1923

Architects:
Lowe & Bollenbaher (Chicago)
A.H. Buckley

Excavation for this Gothic Revival stone church began in 1922. Local architect A.H. Buckley assisted the Chicago firm of Lowe & Bollenbaher in designing the structure.

A prominent art glass window with tracery is set into a pointed arch on the east elevation, and additional paired leaded art glass windows set into concrete surrounds line the nave.

John J. Wolcott Residence

5225 Wyandotte Street
1915

Architect:
Shepard, Farrar & Wiser

Builder:
Joe Hellman

Built for John J. Wolcott, a grain dealer, this two-story brick and stucco house – with its low hip roof and wide bracketed eaves – is an example of the Prairie School style.

The principal architect of the firm that built the house was Charles E. Shepard, who specialized in domestic architecture and designed more than 600 houses in the Country Club and Mission Hills districts.

William H. Collins Residence 16

232 West 52nd Street
1924

Architect:
Edgar G. Faris

Builder:
William H. Collins

This two-and-one-half-story stucco house is an interpretation of the Mediterranean style, typified by its tile roof. Its elaborate three-arched recessed entrance porch is surmounted by a balcony; the supporting brackets have the shape of animal heads.

Another Collins house was built for William Collins' son, Rawlings Collins. It is a beautifully landscaped one-and-one-half-story brick and stucco house erected in 1923 and located at 5717 Wornall Road.

The Peanuts Apartments

5001-5049 Wyandotte Street
1925-1926

Architect:
Wilkinson & Crans

Builder:
H. Kelly

The early residents, in response to the luxurious development to the west (The Walnuts), wryly nicknamed these apartments "The Peanuts." Each of the two-story half-timbered stucco and brick buildings contains four apartments.

Wilkerson and Crans also designed the former Kansas City School of Law building at 913 Baltimore Avenue and the Notre Dame de Sion French Institute at 3823 Locust Street.

The Walnuts Apartments

5049 Wornall Road
1929-1930

Architect:
Boillot & Lauck

Builder:
Charles Ogan Jones

From the first, these Jacobethan-style apartments were intended to be elegant and luxurious, and that is how they remain today more than eight decades later. The three 10-story buildings replaced the Wallace N. Robinson residence, "The Walnuts."

Variegated brick trimmed with Bedford limestone was used for the exterior facades.

Mary Rockwell Hook Residence 19

4940 Summit Street
1925-1927

Architect:
Mary Rockwell Hook

Builder:
Long Construction Co.

These Italian-inspired stone residences were designed by Mary Rockwell Hook for members of her family and herself. Hook took particular delight in the rugged topography, which she preserved and reflected in her designs.

When Hook began her practice in Kansas City, she was turned down by the firm of Wight & Wight, who refused to hire a woman, but she was accepted by Howe, Hoit & Cutler. Later she formed her own business with a partner, Mac Remington.

Mrs. E.D. Hook Residence 20

5011 Sunset Drive
1922-1923

Emily Rockwell Love Residence 21

5029 Sunset Drive
1915

Floyd Jacobs Residence

5050 Sunset Drive
1925

Architect:
Hook & Remington

Builder:
Ward Investment Co.

Seven of the nine Kansas City residences designed
by Mary Rockwell Hook are located in the Sunset Hills
neighborhood. The Ward Investment company developed the area and sold off the flat lots initially, with many
steep, hillside lots remaining. The Company asked Mrs.
Hook to design a home to demonstrate effective hillside
construction. The architect selected for this demonstra-
tion home had to solve not only the problem of hillside
construction, but also to handle the unusual situation of
a double frontage of streets of different elevations and
on a lot of irregular proportions.

Hook masterfully conquered all of these difficulties in the
design of this home and as a result, boosted the sale of
hillside lots. The home was originally the home of Floyd
Jacobs, a member of the law firm of Jacobs and Henderson.

Raymond Starr Residence

5044 Summit Street
1935-1936

Architect:
James F. Terney

Builder:
Joe F. Gier

A young engineering graduate of modest means, Raymond Starr was determined to build a moderately priced yet functional house which incorporated the most modern construction features.

Extensive European travel in the 1920s and 1930s had led Starr to admire the new International Style developed by the Bauhaus practitioners. His residence is possibly the earliest in the city utilizing this design. Placing the garage in the front and locating the living room at the rear overlooking the garden were controversial concepts.

Some of the innovations in the Starr home have become commonplace in residential construction.

Bertrand Rockwell Residence

1004 West 52nd Street
1908-1909

Architect:
Mary Rockwell Hook

As the first of her Kansas City residential designs was nearing completion, Mary Hook, then still Mary Rockwell, planned and superintended the construction of a home for her parents, Mr. and Mrs. Bertrand Rockwell. The Rockwells required a large residence as they and four of their daughters were to live in it.

The house is stylistically quite different from Hook's other Kansas City works, as it possesses an almost classical facade. In other aspects, her personal design idiom is present. The large double verandas on each end of the house, now enclosed, attest to her love of nature. The stage on the third floor is a feature found in almost all of her works. A novel aspect in this house was the construction of a basement garage on the north side of the house, reportedly one of the first garages in the city to be incorporated into the house.

Richard O. Smith Residence

1015 W. 54th Street
1923

Architect:
Horace LaPierre

Builder:
Richard O. Smith

A substantial wrought iron fence surrounds this handsome two-and-one-half-story red brick Neo-Georgian style residence. Particularly notable are the truncated green tile roof and quoined corners.

The house was built for Smith, an executive with the Brockett Cement Company.

Seth E. Ward Residence

26

1032 W. 55th Street
c. 1856-1857

Architect:
Asa Beebe Cross

This Greek Revival style home, originally built in 1858 by trader William Bent, was purchased by Seth E. Ward in 1871 and redesigned and enlarged by architect Asa Beebe Cross.

Ward was a trapper, Santa Fe trader and supplier for the U.S. Army who earned his fortune trading with Native Americans. While the form and massing of the house are Greek Revival, the porch elements reflect early Victorian styling. The exterior of the farmhouse is clad with brick produced from local materials, and Italianate additions such as the veranda modified the original design. The resulting appearance is closer to a high Victorian style than a pure expression of classic Greek Revival.

Some of the fiercest engagements during the Battle of Westport in October 1864 occurred in the farm's east pasture. The house was placed on the National Register of Historic Places in 1978.

Bernard Corrigan Residence

1200 West 55th Street
1912-1913

Architect:
Louis S. Curtiss

Builder:
Bernard Corrigan Construction Co.

Architecturally one of the most striking residences in Kansas City, the profile of this house reflects many characteristics of the work of Frank Lloyd Wright and the Prairie School. On the other hand, its ornamentation reflects the Art Nouveau movement at its height early in the century. The decorative value of curvilinear movement is apparent in both the fanciful and luminous stained glass and the masonry reliefs that adorn the facades. Especially noteworthy is the large art glass window west of the front entrance featuring violet blossoms and the fluttering leaves of a wisteria vine.

The architect, Louis Curtiss, was commissioned to design the house for Bernard Corrigan, a building contractor, street railway developer, and real estate investor. The long span girders and reinforced concrete that Curtiss used in the construction were novel in domestic structures at that time. Corrigan died shortly before the house was completed; consequently his family never occupied it.

Mack Nelson Residence

5500 Ward Parkway
1914

Architect:
Henry F. Hoit

Builder:
J.R. Vansant

This grand residence features a tiled, hipped roof with moderate overhang and wooden brackets (Italian Renaissance influenced), and paired, colossal Corinthian columns on large plinths typical of the Beaux-Arts style. Prominent broken gabled dormers with arched, multi-paned windows break the roof line, and four exterior brick chimneys are situated at the corners of the structure. The interior features a center courtyard lit by a moveable skylight.

The first resident of this home was Mack B. Nelson, president of the Long-Bell Lumber Company.

Charles S. Keith Residence

1214 West 55th Street
1913

Architect:
Shepard, Farrar & Wiser

The Charles S. Keith Residence, located at 1214 W. 55th Street, was designed by the Kansas City architectural firm of Shepard, Farrar & Wiser in 1913 and completed in 1914. The two-and-one-half-story Flemishbond brick, cut-stone and concrete Georgian Revival home is sited on a three-acre lot. Hare and Hare, the nationally prominent Kansas City landscape architecture firm, was responsible for the design of the grounds in 1913.

Charles S. Keith was the president and general manager of the Central Coal & Coke Company when the house was built at a cost of $75,000.

Charles Braley Residence

3 Dunford Circle
1919

Architect:
Hoit, Price & Barnes

Builder:
Long Construction Co.

The Charles Braley house is a Jacobethan Revival style brick and stone mansion. Completed in 1919, the three-story home has multiple gables, buttresses, towering chimneys, detailed windows, and elaborate stonework. The solid and imposing house is one of Kansas City's jewels, designed by prominent architect Henry Hoit and built by the R.A. Long Construction Company.

Charles Braley came to Kansas City in the late 1880s and joined the law firm of Dobson, Douglas and Trimble specializing in corporate, real estate and commercial law. In 1917, Braley was named vice president of the Sinclair Consolidated Oil Corporation plant located in Argentine, Kansas. Braley was very active in civic affairs and was a member of the Blue Hills Country Club, Mission Hills Country Club, and the Mid-Day Club.

James F. Halpin Residence

1226 West 56th Street
1913

Architect:
John W. McKecknie

Builder:
Long Construction Co.

A Renaissance Revival mansion of solid concrete faced with cut stone was erected for James F. Halpin, contractor, real estate operator and one of the builders of the Intercity Viaduct.

Halpin was a partner in the Corrigan Construction Company, which also built the tracks for the old Metropolitan Street Railway Company.

Pendergast Residence

5650 Ward Parkway
1928

Architect:
Edward W. Tanner

Builder:
J.C. Nichols Co.

Although not a textbook example of the French Eclectic style, this residence recognizes certain elements borrowed from that period, including the tall, steeply pitched hipped roof, the casement type windows and dormers set into segmental arched openings, and a segmental entrance embellished with rusticated stonework.

Surface décor includes elaborate brick work, a molded string course, and a tall parapet with a cartouche.

The first resident was Thomas J. Pendergast, vice president of the Ready Mixed Concrete Company.

George E. Nicholson Residence **33**

1028 W. 58th Street
1918

Architect:
Wight & Wight

Builder:
John Reynard

Representative of the Neoclassical style popular in the area is this two-and-one-half-story stucco residence with an imposing tetra style portico. It was built for George E. Nicholson, developer of zinc mines and smelters.

Architects Wight and Wight are known for their designs of the Nelson Gallery-Atkins Museum, City Hall, and the old Children's Mercy Hospital.

Stratford Gardens Homes

1230-1238 Huntington
1926-1928

Architects:
1200 - George M. Siemens
1234 - Elmer Boillot
1238 - Clarence E. Shepard
1241 - Amanda Elizabeth Evans Rivard

The brick and stucco half-timbered Tudor Revival and French farmhouse style has been a perennial favorite in Kansas City, as these spacious residences suggest.

The architect for the house at 1230 Huntington Road, bearing the clay tile chimney pots, was George M. Siemens. The architect for 1234 Huntington Road was Elmer Boillot, the architect for 1238 Huntington Road was Clarence E. Shepard, and the architect for 1241 was Amanda Elizabeth Evans Rivard, who signed her plans "A.E. Evans" to avoid the discrimination at the time of being identified as a woman architect.

Country Club Christian Church   **35**

6101 Ward Parkway
1921; 1924; 1958

Architect:
Root & Siemens

Builder:
John Niel & Son

A richly decorated structure, this church is a prominent landmark on Ward Parkway. Designed in the Gothic tradition, the structure includes massive piers, buttresses, Gothic tracery, and stone coping. In addition, materials of contrasting color and texture enliven the exterior surface. A massive entryway with stone tympanum and a broad spired tower dominate the main (west) façade.

John B. Wornall House

146 West 61st Terrace
1858

This antebellum farmhouse is considered one of the finest and least altered Classic Revival style structures still standing in Kansas City. Built of red brick in 1858, it is distinguished by its two-story high front porch with square columns, steep pediment, recessed second-story balcony, and large central hall. The main façade is symmetrical and each façade has a wide wooden full entablature.

The house was originally part of Wornall's 110 acre farm and served as a field hospital for both Union and Confederate wounded during the Battle of Westport in October 1864. The architect is unknown, but Wornall apparently served as his own contractor. The brick for the house was probably fired on site and the walls are 12 inches thick. The limestone for the foundation, door and window lintels, and the fireplaces was all quarried on or near the farm.

Greenway Terrace Tudor Revivals 37
400 block of Greenway Terrace
1919-1920

Architects:
Arthur H. Buckley & Courtland Van Brunt

Builder:
J.C. Nichols Co.

The architects' intent of the Greenway Terrace subdivision design was to capture the charm of an English streetscape while providing good housing at a relatively low cost. Many houses are of stucco with shingle roofs and decorative half-timbering. The similarity in design is broken by an occasional brick facade or brick trim; thus, the houses are tied together architecturally while still retaining individuality. Until 1917 this area was part of the holdings of the Wornall family.

Wornall Road Baptist Church 38

400 West Meyer Boulevard
1929

Architect:
Felt, Dunham & Kriehn

Builder:
Tilden H. Lishear

Located at the northwest corner of Wornall Road and Meyer Boulevard, this red brick and stone building with white trim, four two-story-tall Corinthian columns on the main façade, and a towering steeple lit at night from within, is a fine example of Georgian colonial church architecture. The west and east façades are each adorned with five two-story-high arched-toped stained glass windows, and the interior sanctuary is set off with a simple clear span ceiling, which is one of the prominent features of the building. "The Church at Brookside," as it is often referred, was constructed in 1930 and replaced a smaller structure. One of the founding members of the congregation was a member of the John B. Wornall family.

Border Star School

6321 Wornall Road
1924-1928

Architect:
Charles A. Smith

Builder:
John Gosling

The central section of this red brick and cut stone Neo-classical school was completed in 1924 and was enlarged to its present size in 1928.

Border Star stands on ground once occupied by a one-room rural school house opened in 1873, which served the area south of Westport for over fifty years, and the present edifice has continuously served the educational needs of residents of the Brookside area for the past ninety years. Its name is derived from an early newspaper in the Kansas City area and suggests a time when the Missouri border was the farthest western border of the continental United States.

Country Club Police & Fire Station **40**

22 West 63rd Street
1917

Architect:
Frederick H. Michaelis

Builder:
J.C. Nichols Co.

One of the first buildings erected in the 63rd and Brookside shopping area was this combination police and fire station. The developer, J.C. Nichols Company, was anxious to provide adequate protection for nearby residential districts, yet wished to house the services in a building which blended into the neighborhood.

St. Peter, Prince of Apostles

715 East Meyer Boulevard
1943-1946

Architects:
Carroll & Dean; Joseph B. Shaughnessy, Sr.

Builder:
J.E. Dunn; John Cahill

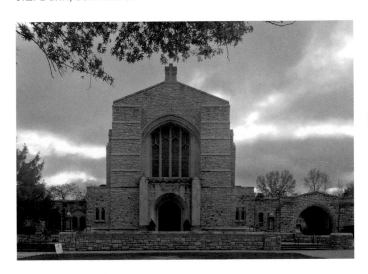

Due to wartime restrictions on building, permission to construct had to first be obtained from the government. Plans by the architects were reviewed by the city's art commission. The church was finally dedicated in 1946.

St. Peter, Prince of Apostles won an American Institute of Architects, Kansas City chapter, award in 1947. Significant features include the main entry set into a ribbed, pointed arch recess, placed within a crenelated portal flanked by massive stone piers, and a porte-cochere located at the west elevation. A pointed arched cloister is located at the east façade.

Sanctuary furnishings were designed by Charlton Fortune of the Monterey Guild, Portsmouth, Rhode Island. Stations of the Cross were designed by John H. Benson.

Armour Hills

Meyer Road to Gregory Boulevard,
Wornall Road to Oak Street

Developer:
J.C. Nichols Co.

J.C. Nichols purchased land that would become the
Armour Hills neighborhood from the Armour family in
1922. When the area was planned, Nichols stipulated
that the homes should be unique, single-family homes.
The neighborhood features a variety of early 20th century
Revival styles, including Tudor, Craftsman and Colonial
Revival that were meant for the middle class of the area.

The neighborhood features Arbor Villa Park at its center
and traffic islands with statuary and fountains, which
were a hallmark of J.C. Nichols subdivision design.
Armour Hills is also well known for the first J.C. Nichols
neighborhood to establish restrictive covenants, which
served as a model for all of the Country Club District.

Country Club
Congregational Church

43

205 West 65th Street
1925-1926; addition 1948

Architect:
Root & Siemens

The Country Club Congregational Church was established in 1923 in response to the church demands of this denomination in a developing neighborhood. The Kansas City Congregational Union purchased the ground for the church and within three years a Neoclassical Revival style building was erected.

Both Ionic columns and Doric pilasters decorate the portico, surmounted by an interesting double pediment. The five-pointed star, which crowns the lantern and cupola of its steeple, has long been the emblem of the church. Opalescent art glass windows, in geometric design, decorate its narthex and nave.

Armour Fields Romanelli Gardens

Wornall Road to Ward Parkway,
Meyer Road to Gregory Boulevard

Developer:
J.C. Nichols Co.

These subdivisions, located south of the Plaza between 65th Street and Gregory, are textbook examples of J.C. Nichols' original design. All three subdivisions sport tree-lined streets, ornamental statuary, and small landscaped parks (such as the lovely Romanelli Park and fountain at the confluence of 69th Street, Edgevale and Wornall roads) all designed to follow and enhance the natural terrain.

These neighborhoods also include Colonial, Georgian, Mediterranean and Italianate styles, as well as homes of the Prairie School of Design.

Southwest High School

6512 Wornall Road
1925-1926

Architect:
Charles A. Smith

Builder:
J. Gosling (1924); Sharp
Brothers Construction Co.

As Kansas City grew to the south, a new high school was needed to meet demands. In 1925, the central portion of the Southwest High School was completed for approximately $300,000. The central portion of the building contained eight classrooms, a temporary gymnasium and domestic science rooms. In 1926, nineteen additional classrooms were added as well as a branch of the public library. The auditorium was completed in 1931 and an additional nine classrooms were added in 1938. A new gymnasium was added to the south in 1962.

The building was designed by Charles A. Smith, the architect of many Kansas City schools, in the Neoclassical style. Another person, Edgar A. Welty, an artist in Smith's office, was responsible for at least a portion of the design. The entrance is distinguished by six Corinthian columns, which support an entablature with dentils. Decorative urns project from the centrally located parapet that tops this grand entrance. Stone belt courses are interspersed between the brick cladding, making this one of the best examples of high-style Neoclassical architecture in Kansas City.

Sixth Church of Christ, Scientist   **46**

400 West 67th Street
1925-1926

Architect:
Charles A. Smith

Builder:
Fisher-Owen Construction Co.

The tract of land for this church was purchased for
$20,500 in June 1923, plans were drawn in 1924, and
construction began on May 11, 1925.

Features of this Late Gothic Revival building include a
double wooden door entry set into a pointed stone arch,
massive art glass windows set into pointed stone arches,
prominent stone buttresses with amortizements, and four
additional entrances. A three-story, crenelated tower is
crowned by a spire that reaches a height of 150 feet and
displays multiple spire lights.

Building costs for the church were estimated at
$226,000.

Kirk B. Armour Farmhouse 47

6740 Pennsylvania Avenue
1898

This seven room Civil War-era farmhouse was the center
of a 600-acre stock farm when it was built. The farm
house had a large wrap-around porch, a white picket
fence, and a dirt road that ran east from the front of the
house to Wornall Road. Members of the Armour family, of meat packing fame, purchased the house and the
farm in the early 1900s. Twenty years later the Armour
family sold the farm to the J.C. Nichols Company, and
by 1926 Nichols opened the farm for residential development.

The "Armour House," was purchased by David W.
Childs, who renovated the structure, replacing the front
porch with twin corner porches on either side of the
main entrance (since lost), and two-story-high Corinthian
columns supporting the front porch and topped with attic
dormer windows.

Walter E. Bixby Residence

48

6505 State Line Road
1935-1937

Architect:
Edward W. Tanner

Builder:
J.C. Nichols Co.

Atop a wooded hillside, this sweeping concrete and stucco home embodies the International style. The concrete foundation rests on a natural rock ledge. and exterior walls are made of concrete blocks surfaced with stucco over metal lathing.

Hare and Hare, landscape architects, designed the hillside where native trees are interspersed with out-croppings of rock. The house was built for Walter Edwin Bixby, Sr., chairman of the board of the Kansas City Life Insurance Company.

Ward Parkway Estates **49**

7200-7211 Jarboe Street
1929

Builder:
Napoleon W. Dible

These half-timbered stucco and brick homes are typical of the hundreds of residences erected throughout the city by Napoleon W. Dible, one of Kansas City's most prolific home builders. Beginning his long business career in 1905, Dible was one of Kansas City's first builders to recognize the economies possible by standardizing floor plans, purchasing materials in quantity, and employing a cadre of skilled workmen.

In addition, Dible always refrained from erecting monotonous rows of identical boxes; he mingled facades and floor plans so as to appeal to a variety of individual preferences.

New Reform Temple (Jackson Telephone Exchange)

50

7100 Main Street
1913

Architect:
Smith, Rea & Lovitt

Builder:
Bert L. Elmer

The former Jackson Telephone Exchange building was converted by the members of the Brookside Methodist Episcopal Church in June 1932. The sire was purchased from the Southwestern Bell Telephone Company. In 1927, when 71st Street was widened as Gregory Boulevard, the building was moved south from its original site to avoid demolition. It was enlarged at that time and was said to be the largest telephone exchange building that had ever been moved in this country without an interruption of service.

Rockhill Gardens

Gregory Street to 75th Street,
Holmes Road to Grand Avenue

Builder:
Napoleon Dible

Developer:
Napoleon Dible

Among the single-family homes built, many were constructed by Napoleon W. Dible during the late 1920s. He was one of Kansas City's first builders to standardize floor plans, purchase materials in bulk, and employ skilled workmen, all part of his effort to make his homes affordable to the average home buyer. Dible is best known for his modified English two-story Tudor made of brick, stucco and stone; dramatically set off in timber frame sections with two or three pronounced gables.

Waldo Water Tower
Tower Park

75th Street and Holmes Road
1919-1920

Builder:
Tifft Construction Co. (Buffalo, NY)
Flint Construction Co.

The Waldo Water Tower, officially called the Frank T.
Riley Memorial Tower is located in Tower Park. This
twelve-sided tower is 134 feet tall, with reinforced concrete walls 12 inches thick, and a capacity of 1 million
gallons. The tower is topped by crenellations and twelve
arched windows. It was constructed using a fourteen-day
continuous pour. The structure was a functioning water
tower from 1920 until 1957. The tower was pictured each
year from 1929 to 1946 in the World Book Encyclopedia
as an early example of reinforced concrete. It was listed
in 1975 as Missouri's first American Water Landmark by
the American Water Works Association, and is on the
National Register of Historic Places.

Waldo Commercial District

Wornall Road & 75th Street

The Waldo commercial district, roughly the six-to-seven block area running from 74th to 77th streets, and Jefferson to Main, became a part of Kansas City in 1909. The annexation was in anticipation of continued growth to the south spurred by the J.C. Nichols Company and numerous home builders. Since building supplies were in great demand, one of the first lumber suppliers in the area was established at Waldo and was fed by a rail line that ran from Westport south along the east side of Wornall Road. Waldo soon became the southern terminus of the Kansas City Streetcar Line. Pitkin Hall, built in 1907, sits on the northwest corner of 75th Street and Wornall and was one of the first commercial buildings in Waldo.

The Waldo Commercial District of today is an eclectic collection of old and new structures, sporting numerous bars, restaurants and locally owned businesses, making Waldo an appropriate companion to the Brookside area to the north.

Alexander Majors Residence

8145 State Line Road
1856; add. 1903

A solid example of a free-hand version of the Greek Revival style farm home, this house was built by Alexander Majors, a partner in the freighting firm of Russell, Majors & Waddell, which thrived on outfitting those preparing to head west on the Oregon or Santa Fe trails.

Majors was the founder of the ill-fated Pony Express in 1860, and helped establish the Kansas City Stockyards. He had become wealthy in the 1850s as a result of hauling supplies to U.S. Army posts all along the Santa Fe Trail. The palatial home was built of wood instead of brick. An overall T-plan, the recessed porch on the main façade that was originally two-stories high, became the centerpiece of his business activity.

The residence was placed on the National Register of Historic Places in 1970 and is now operated as a museum.

Martin City
Hickman Mills
Little Blue Valley

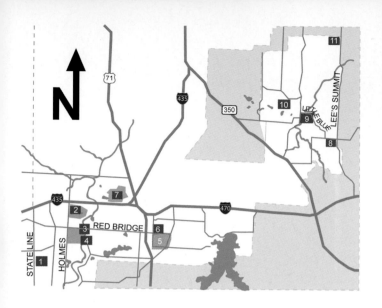

1. New Santa Fe Cemetery and Trail Ruts
2. Mt. Moriah Cemetery Mausoleum
3. Red Bridge
4. Minor Park - Santa Fe Trail Ruts
5. Hickman Mills
6. Hickman Mills Church
7. Oakwood Club - Rule Farm
8. Jackson County's Poor Farm & County Home -
   Patterson Hall (Truman Medical Center Lakewood)
9. Little Blue Township
10. Four Gates Farm
11. White Oak School

Martin City
Hickman Mills
Little Blue Valley

South Kansas City's historic sites and structures tell two stories. The earliest sites recall the region's connection to the Santa Fe Trial and pioneer life, bringing to mind the pioneers whom traveled west in search of the 19th century American dream. The more modern sites, mostly from the early 20th century, demonstrate how the population from a growing metropolis expanded into the countryside in search of a respite from the hustle and bustle of city life. Each of the constituent communities that make up the Southland – Martin City, Hickman Mills, and Little Blue – share a common pioneer past and an eventual Kansas City future.

South Kansas City was pioneer territory throughout much of the 19th century. The Santa Fe Trail played a major role in bringing settlers to the area. The presence of permanent settlements is a testimony to the trail's influence, but little remains of the actual physical trail itself in much of the Kansas City metro area. The major exceptions are in South Kansas City, where original ruts (swales) left by westbound wagon trains are still visible in Minor Park. These tracks are exceedingly rare in the more developed areas of Kansas City. A few miles away, the New Santa Fe Cemetery provides a more macabre reminder of the pioneers. Located on West Santa Fe Trail road just east of State Line, the cemetery site has its own set of original trail swales nearby.

Heading east from the New Santa Fe Cemetery, visitors come to the Red Bridge community. The region draws its name from several bridges built over the Blue River at what is today Red Bridge Road between Holmes and Blue River Road. The current Red Bridge (1933) is the third incarnation; the first was a wood and stone bridge that Colonel George N. Todd built slightly downriver in 1859; the second bridge featured tin construction and stood from 1893 until the construction of the current Red Bridge. Dedicated by Harry S. Truman in January 1933, the current Red Bridge serves as a local marital landmark. Kansas City couples traditionally order custom engraved locks to commemorate their nuptials, then symbolically close the lock on the Red Bridge and toss away the keys.

The other historic places in South Kansas City are an eclectic mix. There's the Oakwood Country Club at Rule Farm, where the Jewish-German Congregation B'nai Jehudah's Progress Club converted a local farm into one of the region's early golf courses. Truman Medical Center's Lakewood Campus, northeast of the Oakwood Club, has a hidden past of its own: the modern hospital stands on the grounds and shares buildings with the former Jackson County's Poor Farm (1851). Mount Moriah Cemetery, on Holmes Road, features a striking mausoleum with an unusual dual purpose. The large Egyptian-themed mausoleum (1926) was built to serve as both a crypt and as a temple for Masonic meetings and rituals. Much like the Mausoleum Temple, there are many hidden architectural and historic gems tucked away in Jackson County's outlying communities.

South Kansas City is large in area but features only a select number of historic sites. Unlike the urban core, the outlying areas in Martin City, Hickman Mills, and Little Blue did not see an explosion of development in the immediate post-Civil War-era. Consequently, their historic and architectural stories are still unfolding.

New Santa Fe Cemetery and Trail Ruts

900-902 West Santa Fe Trail Road
1821-1860

Independence was the leading trailhead for the Santa Fe Trail from 1827-1845. As the trail passed by what is now the New Santa Fe Cemetery, the continual pressure of wagon trains etched indelible marks, or swales, in the ground. The most notable section of the trail now extends from Madison Street to the border of the New Santa Fe Cemetery. The swales vary in length and width, culminating near the middle of the trail segment, where two swales are clearly visible.

The adjacent New Santa Fe Cemetery contains approximately 140 known burials. Though the trail had passed through the surrounding area since 1822, the earliest known internment at the cemetery dates from 1869. The last large scale wagon trains west traveled along the Santa Fe Trail at near the same time that the cemetery had its first internment. Fortunately, between the swales at nearby Minor Park, and those here, the physical evidence of westward migration lives on.

Mt. Moriah Cemetery Mausoleum 2

10503 Holmes Road
1927

Architect:
Robert E. Peden

Mount Moriah Cemetery Mausoleum and Masonic
Temple are striking examples of Egyptian revival style.
Completed in 1927, the stone structure's design was
based on the ancient Egyptian temple at Karnak. The
modern temple's exterior features many Egyptian motifs:
obelisks, sphinx, and winged sun iconography. Papyrus
and lotus flowers – the historic symbols of Lower and
Upper Egypt – adorn the main entrance, and the mauso-
leums' columns feature stylized papyrus capitals.

The mausoleum's connection to Freemasonry helps
explain the preponderance of Egyptian motifs. Built
to serve Kansas City's Mason population exclusively,
Mount Moriah's Mausoleum also contains an active
Masonic Temple Room. Known for their secrecy, Masons
also have a penchant for incorporating ancient iconography into their temples and meeting places. Building
in the Egyptian Revival Style was both an allusion to
hallowed antiquity and participation in a fashionable,
contemporary architectural style.

Red Bridge

Red Bridge Road over the Blue River
1859; 1892; 1933

Architect: Builder:
Richard Wakefield   Jackson County

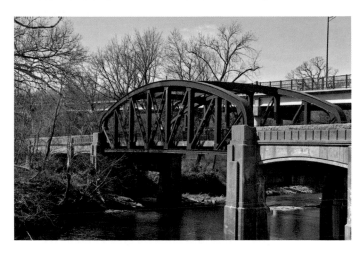

There have actually been three Red Bridges over the
Blue River. George M. Todd, a Scottish stonemason,
constructed the first bridge 1859. Todd's red-painted
bridge featured a wood span supported by stone piers,
located just downstream from modern bridge. Telling of
the conflict gripping the region, Todd would not live to
see the creation of the second or third Red Bridges. A
Confederate guerilla leader under William Quantrill, Todd
was killed in 1864 at the Second Battle of Independence.
Todd's bridge outlasted its creator by some twenty-eight
years. The original was torn down in 1892. The first
replacement bridge was made of steel, and also painted
red, continuing Todd's tradition. The modern Red Bridge,
built by Jackson County during the Great Depression,
opened in 1933. Harry S. Truman was on hand to dedi-
cate the handsome new through arch bridge, made of
concrete and steel with a base faced in red granite.

Minor Park - Santa Fe Trail Ruts   **4**
1821-1865

The Santa Fe Trail swales, also commonly referred to as ruts, are a somewhat unusual inclusion in a book dominated by buildings, bridges, and other structures. The swales testify to the enormous amount of wagon traffic leaving Kansas City and headed west to Santa Fe, Colorado, and Oregon. The number of wagons on the trail varied according to the season, the destination, and the local political environment. The turbulent conflict in the years surrounding the Civil War threatened to end Kansas City's position on the trail.

Of course, not even the war could compete with the change wrought by progress. At the war's end, the continued rise of railroads began to curtail trail traffic. The last large-scale wagon train departed for Santa Fe in the spring of 1866. Subsequent development in the Kansas City metro area, combined with the unyielding power of the weather, threatened to eliminate all physical evidence of the trail. Luckily, the swales in Minor Park offer the curious an opportunity to look at the lasting marks that the age of the horse drawn wagon left on the face of Kansas City.

Hickman Mills

Red Bridge Road & Hillcrest Road

Positioned near the junction of the Santa Fe, California and Oregon trails, Hickman Mills was annexed by the city in 1961. Randall Allen platted the site in 1845, but its name came from Edwin Alfred Hickman who, built a steam-powered grist and saw mill. Its current name was due to a clerical error: When the community applied for a federal post office it was written down as Hickman Mills, instead of Hickman's Mill. While never formally incorporated, the town had a bank, shops, post office, and churches. A.J. King platted "Hickman Orchards" in 1928 on a former orchard as a suburban getaway and one of Kansas City's early exurbs.

Hickman Mills Church

5809 East Red Bridge Road
1920; add. 1930

Thirteen original members founded the congregation in May 1845, at a location near what is now 92nd and Bannister. First known as the Bethlehem Christian Church, the congregation agreed to move to its current location in 1856. Local mill owner Edwin H. Hickman offered the congregation an acre and a half of land to relocate and change their name to Hickman's Mill Christian Church. The church used several different structures between 1856 and 1929, as it frequently outgrew its accommodations and had to construct larger facilities.

Booming Sunday School attendance played a major role in the 1920 decision to construct the current church, a Norman-Gothic, double gable design made of rusticated stone. Other notable features include stone buttresses and through cornice gable dormers. In spite of its much increased sized compared to the preexisting church, the 1929 building was soon overcrowded, and the congregation decided to expand again. The result, a red-brick addition that dates from 1958, housed youth groups and other fellowship activities.

Oakwood Club - Rule Farm 7

9700 Grandview Road
1930

Architect:
Greenebaum, Hardy & Schumacher

The Progress Club, a social society of Kansas City's Congregation B'nai Jehudah, founded the Oakwood Country Club in 1913. Desiring a rural location suitable for constructing a golf course, the Progress Club purchased the William A. Rule farm in 1911. Located in what was then rural Jackson County, the property also included a stone farmhouse that was converted into the first clubhouse. Oakwood outgrew that clubhouse, and in 1929 it was razed to make way for the current clubhouse.

Designed by Greenebaum, Hardy, and Schumacher, and built in an English Tudor Revival Style, the modern Oakwood Clubhouse has a rusticated stone base and a slate roof. Gray half-timbering decorates the structure's predominately-white walls, while playful shed and gable roof dormers accent the roof. The club's ability to fund such an ambitious construction project was particularly impressive during the economic difficulties of the Great Depression.

Jackson County's Poor Farm & County Home - Patterson Hall (Truman Medical Center Lakewood)

16001 Little Blue Road
1908-1911; adds. 1928, 1930, 1982, 1997, 2003

Architects:
Charles Smith & Frank Rea

The site of the Truman Medical Center Lakewood began as an almshouse, to serve people who could no longer take care of themselves, along with a working farm. The farm had 300 acres at its peak. The first permanent brick building was completed in 1890. In 1907 voters approved construction of the 212-bed stone hospital building. The hospital, known as Patterson Hall, was complete in 1911. The Jackson County Home was officially closed in 1971. In 1976 it became part of the Truman Medical Center system.

Little Blue Township

Little Blue and Noland Road

Little Blue is representative of the outlying railroad communities that flourished in Jackson County during the late 19th and early 20th century. In 1881, the community consisted of a store, a school house, a railroad station, and several homes. Much of the community's success was predicated on proximity to the Missouri Pacific Railroad. Communication, for example, required a train, some dexterity, and a bit of luck. Each day, the mail was hung on a post near the town's depot, and mail workers on a passing train would grab the bag with a specially designed pole. Sometimes they bungled the transfer and the residents of Little Blue had no choice but to wait for the next day to re-send their outgoing mail.

Some of the still standing structures in Little Blue include a former two-story railroad hotel, a former combination general store and post office, and a brick-fronted former blacksmith's shop. Incorporated into Kansas City in 1961, Little Blue still feels the rumble of the rails, as Amtrak trains traveling between Kansas City and St. Louis pass by the community several times a day.

Four Gates Farm

13001 Little Blue Road
1927

Architect:
Mary Rockwell Hook

Builder:
Hook & Remington

The Four Gates Farm is a residential farm complex consisting of two buildings and auxiliary structures designed by Mary Rockwell Hook. Noted as one of Kansas City's early and most influential female architects, Hook's designs often featured an eclectic style that attempted to integrate the building into the local landscape. The farm was built for Marvin Gates, scion of an affluent Kansas City family and longtime friend of Hook. Four Gates included a farmhouse, caretaker's house, and a stage for theatrical productions. Four Gates was Hook's last residential design in Kansas City.

Hook situated the main house at Four Gates Farm on the crest of the forty-acre property. Hook's use of large bays of casement windows, decks, and balconies all helped achieve her desired aesthetic: making the exterior landscape integral to the views from the home's interior. For Hook, the home needed to fit seamlessly into the landscape, but it was just as important that the landscape fit into the home.

White Oak School

16021 East US 40

The White Oak School District (No. 54) was established in 1881 on land owned by Dr. William Noland. This red brick Colonial Revival school was an important institution to the Little Blue Valley. Its two distinct entrances with semicircular glass fanlights with a keystone at the top of a brick arch make it stand out along Highway 40. This was a five-room school house with two rooms added to its three in 1949. The school was annexed into the Independence School District in 1961 and closed in 1969. In its last year of operation, it had 89 students in grades one through six.

Northland

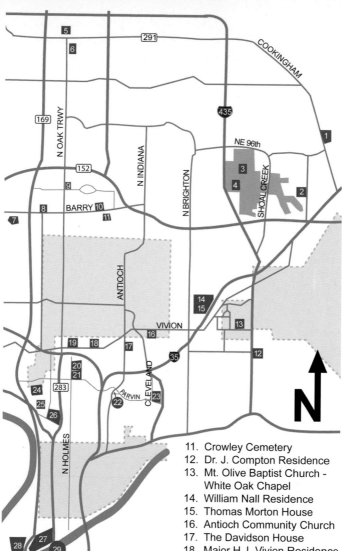

1. Poage-Arnold Residence (Three Gables Farm)
2. Elbridge Arnold Residence
3. Colonel John Thornton House
4. KCMO Radio Station
5. Nashua Commercial Area
6. Barry Community (Cemetery)
7. Gash Cemetery
8. Woods Craftsman Bungalow
9. John Williams Residence
10. Craig-Dolce House
11. Crowley Cemetery
12. Dr. J. Compton Residence
13. Mt. Olive Baptist Church - White Oak Chapel
14. William Nall Residence
15. Thomas Morton House
16. Antioch Community Church
17. The Davidson House
18. Major H.J. Vivion Residence - Ben Foster Residence
19. Vernacular Limestone Residence
20. Russell Residence
21. Prather Spring
22. Montgomery Residence
23. Stuart Perkins Residence
24. Frank Bott Residence
25. Waterworks Park
26. Harlem District
27. Trans World Airlines Admin Offices
28. ASB Bridge

Northland

The history of the Northland is one that combines multicultural stories and a struggle for identity among the
many settlers of the land. A continuous effort to preserve
the legacy of these native cultures, both pre-historic and
historic, remains a priority. Sites such as those at Line
Creek Park were listed on the 1970 National Register for
Historic Places because of their significant artifacts and
relics. These sites contain objects related to the pre-historic Native American Hopewell civilization that inhabited Line Creek Valley from 200 B.C. to 500 A.D. More
recently, traditional cultural sites requiring identification
and preservation have been threatened by development
pressure throughout the fast-growing Northland.

In 1996 construction of the Line Creek Community Center yielded artifacts from the early inhabitants and raised
awareness about the threat of development on richly historic sites. A proposed apartment development adjacent
to Line Creek Park (which could have impacted these
sites) prompted a coalition of civic leaders and historians
to preserve the integrity of the site. In addition, residents
of the area as well as Native American groups have
made it their priority to protect and preserve the cultural
histories of the Northland.

The three districts in the Northland (1, 2 and 4) share
similar histories as well as geographic location, located
within Clay and Jackson Counties. In 1822, Clay County
became an official trading post that outfitted pioneers
and travelers heading west. In 1836 the Federal Government purchased the land west of Clay Country from
the Iowa, Sac, and Fox tribes allowing the creation of
what is now Platte County. Permanent Euro-American
settlers as well as African-Americans arrived after 1820
in Clay County and began farming. The surrounding
Jackson and Platte Counties were settled in 1825 and

1837, respectively. A majority of these settlers migrated from southern states like Kentucky, Tennessee, Virginia, and North Carolina, and they brought with them southern farming traditions such as slave-based agricultural work to produce the cash crops hemp and tobacco. Other early residents came from southern settlement communities in Illinois, Indiana, and Ohio.

As development slowly continued it became evident that communities such as Barry, Gashland, Winnwood, Avaondale, Nashua, Antioch, Randolph, Birmingham, and Minneville all shared the common problem of access to one another and Kansas City. Divided by the Missouri River, only a small ferry in the riverfront town of Harlem provided transportation to and from the Northland. In 1869, the Hannibal Bridge was built in hopes of increasing development of the land north of the river, but this proved unsuccessful. Later in 1885, W.E. Winner, a prominent Kansas City land developer, formed a corporation which bought 10,000 acres of Clay County land at $93 per acre hoping to provide industrial plant sites and low-cost housing for workers. Unfortunately, the 1880s real estate crash prevented Winner's plans and any further development of the Northland.

Although real estate development was brought to a standstill, railway traffic continued thanks to the Chouteau Bridge (ca. 1887, and replaced in December 2001 due to structural problems.) In 1886 it was decided that a rail line extending the Chicago Milwaukee and St. Paul Railway would be constructed from Ottumwa, Iowa, to Kansas City, subsequently increasing the growth of the Northland. This growth and development was furthered in 1911 with the completion of the Armour, Swift, and Burlington Bridge (now Heart of America Bridge), which opened up the area for easier access. The economic growth of the Northland resulted in a rapid decrease of the farming population in 1900, though the land itself remained as farmland through the 1960s.

As Kansas City grew it began annexing parts of the Northland. The first of these annexations occurred on January 1, 1950, and included 19.7 square miles located south of Gladstone between the Platte County line and the Birmingham Bottoms. This annexation was partly orchestrated by the city manager from 1940-1959, L.P. Cookingham. Following the 1950 annexation, Gashland area, Shoal Creek area, and the present Kansas City International Airport (KCIA) area were effectively annexed on January 1, 1959, and 1962. Opened in 1972, KCIA spurred suburban and commercial development in the Northland. The location was decided upon because the industrial growth in the area would act as a buffer between the airport and the surrounding property owners. Sprawling 9,500 acres, KCIA ranks as one of the largest airports in the nation with available acreage.

The districts north of the river continue to expand commercially and residentially. During the 1980s and 1990s, the 1st and 2nd districts of the Northland saw a pronounced suburban expansion that continues to grow. Over the past 20 years, the Shoal Creek Tax Increment Financing Plan (TIF), implemented in 1994, has stimulated residential, commercial and recreational use within the redevelopment area. Housing options such as Briarcliff West and Tremont Manor (luxury homes and integrated retail/commercial businesses) and retail shopping and dining destinations such as Wilshire Plaza, Zona Rosa, and Burlington Creek provide amenities for a population that has grown from approximately 2,000 people in 2000 to nearly 28,000 in 2016. Employment centers continue to thrive in the surrounding KCIA and

Interstate 29 area. In its modern context, the Northland is a thriving part of Kansas City that provides international transportation, commercial businesses, and an abundance of residential communities outside of the city's urban core. Less tangible are the multicultural histories of the area that require preservation and care. It is the centuries of history and ethnicities that inhabited the area that truly make the Northland an integral part of Kansas City.

Poage-Arnold Residence (Three Gables Farm)

1

9550 NE Cookingham Drive
c. 1824; add. 1870

The Poage-Arnold house is a rare example in western Missouri of a vernacular Gothic Revival brick masonry farm house. The first-story rear (north) two rooms were constructed c. 1824 by Andrew and Nancy Poage, while the front one-and-a-half story Gothic Revival portion was built c. 1860 by Thomas and Martha Arnold; together these two sections form an L-shaped building. In the 1940s, a second story was added over the Poage portion, and a two-story frame section added on the east side within the ell. While there have been some alterations to the house, it still conveys its significance as an early farmstead and is a good example of a vernacular Gothic Revival house.

Elbridge Arnold Residence

8900 NE Flintlock Road
1854

Architect:
Frederick Myers

Builder:
Thomas Morrison

This two-story red brick Greek revival style house was built on a 160-acre farm. It is familiarly known as "Woodneath," a name acquired around 1870 during the ownership of Presley L. Moore, because of the numerous shade trees. It is believed the interior bricks were "burned" on the site while the exterior bricks were purchased in Liberty, Missouri. An acetylene lighting system was used until 1931, when electricity was installed.

Colonel John Thornton House 3

7000 NE Barry Road
1829

Colonel John Thornton and his family were one of the
early settlers of Clay County. Thornton was a military
officer, judge, state legislator, hemp planter, miller, and
ferry owner. The Thornton Mansion was originally built
in 1829 in sight of the Missouri River in southern Clay
County. This building, reconstructed in Hodge Park, is
all that remained of the large farm of this Clay County
pioneer. Brick – made on the original site by slaves –
and local timber make up the materials for the house.

KCMO Radio Station

400 NE Cookingham Drive
1947

The radio station KCMO 810 completed this broadcasting station in 1947. Its Moderne style, also known as "streamline Moderne," has a horizontal orientation. The building has curved flat aluminum clad awnings and glass block, which are common in this style. Five towers are located in the field behind the building. The station is currently used by WHB, but the faint outline of the KCMO letters can be seen on the building.

Nashua Commercial Area

11517 North Oak Trafficway
c. 1900

Nashua is located at the northern-most point of North Oak Trafficway. It was named by Willard E. Winner, an early developer of the northland who moved to the area in the 1800s and was a native of Nashua, Iowa. Like the towns of Gashland, Winner, and Armory, Nashua was located along the Quincy, Omaha and Kansas City rail line. Nashua served the surrounding agricultural areas. It was a town that boasted a post office, five grocery stores, a bank, hardware store, lumberyard, garage, poultry house, livery barn, blacksmith shop, drug store, restaurant, hotel, church, and a physician. It was annexed into Kansas City in 1962 and as the city grew, many of these businesses closed or moved south to more populated areas. There are still parts of the old commercial area including the two-story commercial building at 11517 N Oak built around 1900.

Barry Community (Cemetery)

1317 NW Barry road
c. 1840

Barry, settled in the 1820s, is an unincorporated community in Kansas City North straddling the Clay County-Platte County line northeast of Gladstone. The town began as a trading post for Sac and Fox Indians and was named for William Taylor Barry, appointed postmaster general under President Andrew Jackson. A post office was established in 1829, the only stop for stagecoaches between Liberty Landing in Missouri and Fort Leavenworth in Kansas.

Founded officially in 1840, the Barry Cemetery (east of the well) includes graves that date to the 1830s. The earliest legible date is 1815.

Gash Cemetery

398 NW Barry Road
c. 1839

Members of pioneer families, including the Daniel Carpenter and Joseph Gash families, are buried in this small cemetery. The community of Gashland, named for Joseph Gash, developed as a result of the marketing of farm produce. This produce from orchards, berry fields, and vineyards located near the cemetery stimulated the growth of Gashland.

An early marker in this neighborhood cemetery shows the 1839 burial date of Thaddius Gash, son of Joseph Gash.

Woods Craftsman Bungalow

400 NE 88th Street
c. 1937

This stone Craftsman bungalow is a good example of this popular style that was built by many homeowners in the early 20th century. The Craftsman style became popular from the work of Greene & Greene, two brothers that practiced in Pasadena, California, from 1894 to 1903. Craftsman bungalows were squat and spoke to the landscape having low pitched roofs, exposed rafters, and natural materials like wood, stone and brick. This house was built outside the town of Nashua, which was annexed into the city in 1963. This house was owned by Harry T. and Madge Woods at that time.

The 1940 U.S. Census listed homeowner Harry Woods as a postal clerk.

John Williams Residence

1116 NE Barry Road
c. 1833

This two-story white clapboard house conceals the
original log cabin built by John Williams around 1833.
Williams, who built the house for his bride, was one of
five sons who came west with their widowed mother in
1827; the family stopped here when the woods became
too thick for them to travel further.

The clapboard exterior was added ca. 1850, and additional alterations were made in a 1910 remodeling. This
is one of the first houses constructed on the site of what,
in 1878, became Gashland. The land was annexed by
Kansas City in 1959.

Craig-Dolce House

1333 NE Barry Road
c. 1858

In the year 1827, many pioneer families migrated from Kentucky and settled the Gashland area. The Craig-Dolce house is located on Barry Road, the main road to the town of Barry on the Clay and Platte County line. James Craig purchased this land and laid the foundations for the new house on the site of the original four-room house and the adjacent slave quarters on the property. Rock was quarried locally and clay was excavated by slaves to mold and bake bricks for its construction. Beams, plank floors and timber siding were hewn from nearby oak trees. Shortly after the end of World War I a new owner constructed the large front portico.

Crowley Cemetery

7575 NE 48th Street

Among those buried in this small cemetery are several Clay County pioneers, including James Crowley, an American soldier who served in the Continental Army under General George Washington in the Revolutionary War. His tombstone reads: "Va. Mil. Rev. War. He was at Yorktown when Lord Cornwallis surrendered."

Across the road at 7474 Northeast 48th Street is the T.M. Rogers Cemetery, which also contains the graves of early Clay County settlers.

Dr. James Compton Residence

5410 NE Oak Ridge Drive
1829

The native oak trees that grow here in abundance gave Oak Ridge Farm its name. Until 1954 this clapboard house, now a restaurant, remained in the hands of the Compton family, descendants of James Howard Compton, who came to Missouri from Virginia in the 1830s. Compton married a local girl, Mary Ann Wirt, in 1840 and four years later the couple bought this house. Having been enlarged over the years to suit the occupants' needs, the house has been built around a cabin constructed in 1829.

Mt. Olive Baptist Church - White Oak Chapel

5410 NE Oak Ridge Drive
c. 1914

The church building was moved to this location on the grounds of the Dr. James Compton Residence from an area around North Brighton and NE Vivion Road in 1996. The church is the only known surviving example of the African-American White Oak community. The community developed in the late 1880s on land given to a group of former slaves and their descendants by Fountain Waller, a slave owner. Waller's will left 15 1/2 acres to two brothers who were his slaves. The community that grew up on the land included residences, a two-story lodge/school building, a cemetery and a church. The church served as the center of social and religious activities for African-American families within a 5-mile radius. Congregant Horace Hickman built the church in 1914 using lumber sawn at the nearby mill of Nat Murray, another church member. The lodge/school burned in 1973, and the cemetery, while extant, has no markers. Mt. Olive Baptist Church was moved to its current location and restored through the efforts of the Friends of Sacred Structures.

William Nall Residence

6911 NE 53rd Street
c. 1832

Mourning Harrison and William Nall began construction of this house after they came to Clay County from Kentucky in 1832. Like many of the early large landholders in Clay County, Nall had nine slaves in 1860. The Nall house is a good example of an I-house. This vernacular form is two stories tall, with a central hall, two rooms wide and one room deep. The porches and chimneys varied by region. The Nall house has a two-story porch with a gable roof and the front façade is clad in brick.

Thomas Morton House

3601 NE Vivion Road
c. 1918

Thomas Morton came from Kentucky in 1842, beginning his home as a log house. For three generations this home remained in the Morton family. Morton eventually gave the land for the Antioch Christian Church.

The log house to the west was moved by later owners from the original house. The main house on this 15-acre parcel dates to 1918. It is a classic colonial revival house with a full-width two-story front porch. There are also six other buildings on the property including a large barn.

Antioch Community Church

4805 NE Antioch Road
1859

The original log church erected in 1859 survives under a white clapboard exterior. It was founded in 1853 as a Campbellite congregation by Reverend Moses Lard.

The church, built by the members, retains the two front doors marking separate entrances for men and women.

Directly south of the church is the Anti-Horse Thief Building, built c. 1880. This structure served as the headquarters for the Sugartree Grove Protection Association, organized around 1873, as a citizens group for protection against horse and cattle theft.

The Davidson House 17

1330 NE Vivion Road
c. 1860

This vernacular farm house is located on Vivion Road, the main east-west section road when it was built. The two-story house is a T-shape with a gabled roof and wide cornice molding. Though the house has few decorative details, its focal point is the three-sided bay on the first floor.

Like many farmhouses, the original builder adopted elements from his own traditions as well as popular forms of the era. This type of architecture, known as Vernacular, did not rely on formally schooled architects, but the materials, design skills and traditions of local builders.

This particular house was owned by the Davidson family for many years. The 1914 Clay County Atlas identifies 1330 NE Vivion as the home of William Campbell Davidson, the son of James Oscar Davidson, one of the early settlers of Clay County. William was an attorney in Kansas City before returning to the farm with his brother, Ernest.

Major H.J. Vivion Residence - Ben Foster Residence

700 NE Vivion Road
1947

Architect:
Robert E. Jenks

Builder:
H.B. Smith; Tom McVey

This Colonial Revival house replaced the original 1867 House built by Major Harvey Jackson Vivion, from whom Vivion Road gets its name. Ben Foster and Sheffa Vivion Foster built the current house after a fire destroyed the original after WWII. The house is an excellent example of the Colonial revival style, with its hipped roof, ionic columns on the west and south portico, nine over nine and six over six double-hung windows and overall symmetrical design. It was deeded to the Midwest Baptist Seminary by Sheffa.

Vernacular Limestone Residence **19**

4323 North Holmes Street

The vernacular limestone house is a good example of native materials used on a traditional form. Vernacular architecture is based on locality, which means using local construction materials and local traditions. The building design relies on skills and traditions of local builders, not formally trained architect. This two-story house has a central entry and is symmetrical, similar to the popular Colonial Revival style, but the stone cladding and brick accenting the windows make it a local vernacular adaptation. This area of Clay County in the Gallatin Township was annexed by Kansas City in 1950 and the house was owned by Lyle H. Bean, an insurance adjuster at that time

Christopher and Mary Russell Residence

4301 North Holmes street
c. 1878

This brick Italianate house was built on land first settled by Andrew and Mourning Russell. The Russells came from Tennessee to Missouri in 1817, and to Clay County in 1821. Andrew Russell built the first road extending from Liberty to his place in Clay County now known as Russell Road. Christopher M. Russell, born in 1841, was the next to possess the land, and he built the house in about 1878. Turner C. Russell, his son, owned the house until his death in 1948. After being vacant for a number of years, it was restored as part of the Golden Oaks senior housing project.

Prather Spring

2200 NE 39th Terrace

A small fieldstone building marks Prather Springs, believed to have been used by Indians and early settlers. The land here was granted in 1838 to Baruch Prather by President Martin Van Buren. Prather came to Clay County in 1831 from Kentucky with his brother John. Baruch bought land for $1.25 an acre, including Prather Hill, the area from Antioch Road to the Paseo Midtown Freeway and from Russell Road to Northeast 36th Street. In 1930 a pressure system piped water from this spring to approximately 20 houses up the hill. The use of the spring was discontinued when Kansas City annexed the property and supplied water.

Montgomery Residence

3845 North Cleveland Avenue
c. 1870

The Montgomery Residence is located in the settlement known as Moscow and was named for its builder. This brick I-house has double-hung windows with brick voussoirs. A unique front porch with a room with a gable roof and fish-scale shingle siding defines the front of the house. In 1885, Moscow had a population of 150 and had two churches, a mill, general stores, and a shop. As the ASB Bridge was completed, more housing in the area followed and it was annexed into Kansas City in 1950.

Stuart Dutton Perkins Residence 23

3945 North Briarcliff Road
1938; add. 1955

Developer:
Stuart Dutton Perkins

This stone Cape Cod was built by Stuart Dutton Perkins, the developer of the Briarcliff subdivision. His original career was as a farmer in North Kansas City until he was drafted in World War I. He continued farming after he returned, but by 1930 began selling real estate. Perkins was the president of the Hillside and Hampton Securitas Company and the Perkins Farms and Perkins Dairy.

The Old Briarcliff subdivision design has lots that allowed for wider and shallower houses accommodating the increasing importance of the automobile in suburban life with garages and carports becoming important design elements that created new horizontal house types, like the Cape Cod and Ranch styles. The subdivision also exhibits designs that closely follow the layouts introduced by the Federal Housing Administration in the 1930s that called for long curvilinear blocks, cul-de-sacs, and courts. It also included the arrangement of similarly designed houses in multiple variations to avoid monotony of "tract" housing and to create the feeling of informal village streets.

Frank Bott Residence

3640 North Briarcliff
1959-1962

Architect:
Frank Lloyd Wright

Builder:
S.R. Brunn Construction Co.

One of Wright's last designs before his death in 1959
is this low, sweeping, hillside residence built on Waterworks Hill. The walls of the three-tier structure are of native stone and 2 1/2 feet thick with a cantilevered sheet
metal roof painted "Taliesin Turquoise."

The extensive use of glass enclosing the living room
provides a spectacular view of the skyline of Kansas City
and the bend of the Missouri River. The house is said to
exemplify one of Wright's maxims: "No house should be
built on a hill. It should be of the hill."

Waterworks Park

3392 North Oak Trafficway
1936

Waterworks Park began in 1931 as an extra-curricular activity for employees of the water treatment plant. Using leftover funds and supplies, workers carved out a park below the bluffs of the Briarcliff area. After its completion in 1936, the park offered recreational areas, benches, picnic tables, extensive landscaping, and a small spring-fed lake for swimming during the summer and skating during the winter.

During World War II, Waterworks Park closed for security purposes, and the pine benches were removed for use as lumber. The park reopened in 1950, facing eight years' worth of neglect. The park slowly began to be restored, with renovated lighting, picnic areas, landscaping, and general repairs. Today, Waterworks Park is home to a rigorous disc golf course as well as the Remembered Angels Memorial.

Harlem District

ASB Bridge to Hannibal Bridge,
Missouri River to North Kansas City
c. 1836

Maple, cottonwood, and elm trees shaded the small frame houses that lined the streets of this riverfront community, whose history goes back as far as that of Kansas City. For a variety of reasons, Kansas City grew while Harlem, which "once had a school, hotel, saloons, gas stations, churches, a livery stable, a physician and drugstore, a large grocery store, a post office and a jail," remained a settlement. The construction of bridges from Kansas City over the Missouri River helped seal the fate of Harlem and prevented its growth. Early-day Harlem, though, plagued with floods, was a pastoral place; its economy centered on the ferry boat trade. In 1836, a trader named Peter Roi established a river ferry from Harlem to what is now Main Street in Kansas City. From then until 1911 ferry boats brought the world to Harlem and travelers from the North to Kansas City. Fishing was Harlem's other industry until the late 1930s, when the Missouri River became increasingly polluted.

Trans World Airlines Offices 27

10 Richards Road
1931

Architect:
Alonzo Gentry

Builder:
S. Patti Construction Co.

A stylized eagle symbolizing flight embellishes the north facade of this orange brick, two-story Art Deco building with adjoining 400 foot hangar. Land for the airport was selected in 1927 and dedicated the same year by Charles A. Lindbergh, who flew his "Spirit of St. Louis" to Kansas City for the ceremony. Two factors in the early 1930s contributed to the growth of aviation in the city. Kansas City was chosen as the headquarters of Transcontinental and Western Air, Inc., and United States postal officials readjusted the cross-country air mail route so all air mail between Los Angeles and New York would pass through Kansas City.

A.S.B Bridge

2nd & Locust streets
completed in 1911

Designer:
Waddell & Harrington, Consulting Engineers

Builder:
McClintic-Marshall Construction Co. (Pittsburgh)

Packing houses and railroad interests joined forces to finance construction of the 4,000-foot Armour-Swift-Burlington Bridge across the Missouri River at 2nd and Locust Streets. Although Congress had authorized such a bridge as early as 1887, the project failed to get under-way for more than 20 years.

The A.S.B. design permitted the lower deck carrying railroad traffic to telescope into the upper part leaving the top vehicular deck undisturbed. Dr. John A. L. Waddell, a Kansas City resident from 1886 to 1920, invented the vertical-lift span. A widely known authority on bridge design, he remains a little-known figure in Kansas City where he designed the 12th Street Viaduct, the Intercity Viaduct, and the 15th Street Viaduct over the Blue River.

Index

Lost Properties

American Royal Building, 23rd & Wyoming Streets
Armour Home, 2119 Tracy Avenue
Anderson Skelly Station, 220 West Pershing Road
Beacon Hill Congregational Church, 2400 Troost Ave.
Commercial Building, 1221 Main Street
Commercial Building, 2535 Guinotte Avenue
Commercial Building, 2715-2717 Rochester Street
Delbert Davis Service Station, 940 West 8th Street
Double Cottage, 713 North Chestnut Avenue
E. H. Zirkle Sheet Metal Company, 3418 East 27th Street
Fire Station No. 14, 2504 East 6th Street
General Hospital, 24th & Cherry Street
Irving School, 2404 Prospect Avenue
Israel Link House, 5905 NW Cookingham Drive
Prospect Avenue Congregational Church, 2844 Prospect
      Avenue
Residence, 816 Forest Avenue
Residences, 1200 Pennsylvania Avenue
Residence, 1607 Belleview Avenue
Residence, 3742 Genessee Street
Row Houses, 522-528 Elmwood Avenue
Rufus S. Shaffer Residence, 720 East 48th Street
Russell Stover Candy Store, 1201 East Linwood
      Boulevard
St. Francis Seraph Catholic Church, 809 North Agnes
      Avenue
St. Luke's A.M.E. Church and Parsonage, 4260
      Roanoke Road
Stockyards, 18th & Genessee Streets
West End Hotel, 1619 Genessee Street